Living
the
Posh Mom
Life

The
Fun, Fabulous
and
Fashionable
Guide to Motherhood

Amy Nebens and Jara Negrin

SOURCEBOOKS, INC.®
NAPERVILLE, ILLINOIS

Published by Sourcebooks, Inc.
P.O. Box 4410, Naperville, Illinois 60567-4410
(630) 961-3900
Fax: (630) 961-2168
www.sourcebooks.com

Library of Congress Cataloging-in-Publication Data

Nebens, Amy M.
  Living the posh mom life : the fun, fabulous, and fashionable guide to
motherhood / Amy Nebens and Jara Negrin.
     p. cm.
  ISBN-13: 978-1-4022-0899-7
  ISBN-10: 1-4022-0899-5
  1. Mothers. 2. Motherhood. I. Negrin, Jara. II. Title.

HQ759.N434 2007
646.70085'2--dc22

                                        2007001794

Printed and bound in the United States of America.
BG 10 9 8 7 6 5 4 3 2

Dedication from Jara

To my children, Sam and Hayley, my little loves who fill my heart every time we hug, laugh, and you utter the word "mom." I live for times with the two of you.

To my mother, Phyllis, who was an uber-Posh Mom back when there were few who roamed the earth and continues the legacy to this day.

To my mother-in-law, Rachel, who decreed, "You could be a great writer," with only birthday card messages I had scrawled as proof. A better M-I-L could not be had.

To my aunt Joan, who urged me to not to let my dreams go by the wayside. Thank you for your unending devotion.

To my "mental soul mate" and partner, Amy, I'm filled with appreciation and happiness that we did this project together. I treasure the late nights, laughter, and lentils we shared and look for more of it in the future.

Finally, to my true love, Russell, my husband, who not only helped me become a Posh Mom, but who also makes me the luckiest lady that walks. Your unconditional love for me and dedication to my happiness is all I ever dreamed of.

—Jara Negrin

Dedication from Amy

For the sweetest, most loveable joys in my life, Sydney, Peyton, and Brady—you are my everythings. I feel so lucky to be your mom. Your smiles, giggles, and delicious kisses are my inspirations to be my most posh every day.

For my mom, Iris, you instilled in me that posh is from the inside out, and you are the most wonderful example of a mother a girl could ever look up to.

For my sister, Joy, I have loved taking the parallel path of motherhood with you—you keep my poshdar on track, and laugh with me whenever and wherever.

For my M-I-L, Irene, as a five-time mom, you've taught me so much. I revel in your delight watching this book come to be.

For my partner, Jara, here's the light at the end of the tunnel of wee-hour phone marathons, snagging the best tables at Starbucks, and the funniest moments ever—and boy do we need our shades! So thrilled we did this together.

And to my prince charming, Edward, for offering love, support, and many a late-night ear, once again—I am so blessed to have you beside me. You are the absolute poshest dad (and hubby) I know.

—Amy Nebens

Contents

Introduction

Posh is a state of mind. It's an inner gusto and a personal philosophy that makes you fabulous, from your sense of self to your sense of style, and everything big or bitty in between.

Living the Posh Mom Life is far from an intro to motherhood (you're already way in, girl). Instead, it's a guide for all moms: the formerly free-wheeling and childless posh gal who morphed into plain Jane mom and needs a lift up and out, the mom who would throw herself under a train for her kids but lacks even a speck of social savoir-faire and fashion sense, and the mom who looks like she just stepped off the runway and who pooh-poohs good-bye kisses for fear of smudging her lipstick. It's even for the happening, cool mom who craves pointers on how to keep her groove in full swing. This guidebook was written for all modern mothers: you hip, confident, and stylish women who face your own challenges and triumphs every day. It's for any mom who is posh at heart and wants to find or fine-tune her most remarkable self.

Contrary to popular belief (and dictionary definitions), posh is not about being elegant or highfalutin'. And the only thing it has in common with perfect is the first letter—posh is *not* perfect, it's just put-together. In a mom, posh is her inner strength to continually want, expect, and strive for the best in everything for herself and her family, whether it's how she tenderly nurtures her children and finds them the hottest new mini sneakers or how she ekes out ten minutes with her favorite magazine and then sneaks out to shop from the pages. And even though the word *posh* was born in Britain ("port out, starboard home" referencing the most desirable cabins in transoceanic sailings), that doesn't mean England has a corner on the market. Take their Posh Spice Girl. She was thought posh for her pouty look— nobody even knew if she had a posh persona or not. But the Posh Mom is all about persona—and pouts, pants, and playing London bridges falling down. Not one to think she's got it all coming to her, she doesn't just go through life living, she lives for life and all the amazing things that make up hers: her delicious offspring who make her mom, as well as the guy she adores, the home she loves, the dear social circle she cultivated, and the career she carved out.

More About Posh Mom

She's hip. She's fabulous. She's a mom—even if she doesn't look it. The Posh Mom (referred to as PM on occasion from here on in) is the mother of the new millennium, extending her sensational pre-kid life to include those miniature beings who have rocked her world (in the most amazing ways!).

Pre-kids, the posh girl was hip, savvy, and sensational (at home, at work, at a cocktail party), and giving birth gave her something way more than fat ankles—it gave her the goods to be a modern mom raising the bar on raising her kids. You know her. You marvel at her. You spot her across the parking lot at drop-off, and you can't peel your eyes away because she's got it all together: she's a devoted parent, a loyal friend, a social diva, and she always looks so damn good. Oh, yeah, and every mom wants to be her. How could they not?

The Posh Mom is a rogue, modern woman—confident, capable, and constantly making a good faith effort to be put-together from the inside out. She had, has, has on hold, or has a vision for a happening career, is well traveled, well-informed, well read (fiction, nonfiction, and, of course, the latest fashion and beauty mags), *and* well heeled (and not just with Manolos). She is the same person she was before reading the "positive" result on the pregnancy test (except for a few stretch marks a little cocoa butter would cure). Sure, she used to dine out whenever and wherever, have sex anytime and anywhere, spoil silly only herself and her mate (and her best posh pal on her birthday), and didn't think it could get any better. But it did. Having kids didn't squash her sense of self, nor did it send her style and savvy into storage—it sent it into overdrive.

For the Posh Mom, the word *mother* may be a bit retro, conjuring up images of irons, minivans, aprons (a PM may own one—fitted and fashionable—but is equally eager to order in), and, dare we say it, mashed banana slime in her hair (as if!). Don't get us wrong, the PM has a deep adoration and respect for her grandmother, mother, and even a dear aunt or two, but she's oh-so distinct from her traditional counterparts. Maybe the Posh Mom was graced with divine genes, or maybe she gathered her intuition along the way. Whatever the case, today's PM certainly didn't learn her ways from the typical role models of generations past, whether she was the long-ago martyr mom awash in sacrifice or the more recent soccer mom phenom. But the PM certainly doesn't turn up her nose at those who came before her, either.

Today's PM is actually the anti-snob, a smart cookie who has more than changed with the times and who is taking those old roles and making them her own. She's not stuck at home in the kitchen anymore—unless she wants to be. And if she's into cooking, she makes it rock (turning up the music, pouring a glass of wine, or poring over a favorite celeb's cookbook). She doesn't let carpooling to practices mean focusing solely on the athletes in her charge, either. Once her precious packages have been delivered to the field, she gets down to her own business of compiling tomorrow's shopping list and returning phone calls on her Blackberry while sending the cursory eyebrow wave that says "hello but don't bother me right now" to gossiping gals in neighboring cars.

Being posh is not just about how she looks or what she wears, nor is it about basking in the glory of other people's opinions. Her smooth attitude stems from her soul, where her confidence lives and breeds—the compliments, flattery, and around-town fame are by-products she enjoys but certainly never fished for. Some might think posh is just snobbery, aloofness, or polished on the surface—so not. It's confidence, thoughtfulness, sensitivity, fun-loving joy, and free-thinking ideas, and therefore sought after on every volunteer list, party list, playdate list, and emergency list.

But she's not foolish enough to think she can do it all—Poshie knows that some things have just got to go. So she puts on her posh face, whenever and wherever she can—because she looks and feels better when she does. And no PM works herself into a tizzy thinking she has to be posh 24/7—she leaves that to the scripted stunt doubles in Hollywood who have at least fifteen takes (not to mention a makeup and wardrobe team) to get it right.

Don't confuse realistic expectations, though, with moms who are not at all posh, such as those who have chosen to be disheveled schleppers of their offspring, having abandoned all of their pre-kid interests in the interest of raising children. They've got nothing for themselves, nothing to share with others, and nothing to pass down to their children—nothing posh in that. Then there's the antithesis to this empty mom, who's no more posh than she. Self-centered mom hasn't traded in one iota of her non-mom life—adoring has nothing to do with her kids, it means coveting the fashions she sees in the windows of favorite department stores or setting off to study yoga with a guru in her continued quest for perfect tranquility, while her children are at home anxious for her return.

It's a tough balance to find, but the Posh Mom doesn't conform to all the pressure, and she doesn't jibe with any distorted pictures of parenthood. She's driven to sustain an equilibrium for herself and her family so nobody gets the raw end of the deal. And she carries it off with a poise that no matter her given name, people want to shout out, "Go, Grace!"

The Posh Mom Movement

When did this Posh Mom movement dig in its high heels? There's always been posh out there, but never has it been as mainstream as today. Starting in the late nineties, it began brewing, with new moms everywhere rising up and refusing to relinquish their former fab selves. It was born out of an obvious and fortunate result of a generation of women who abandoned the idea that they needed to get married and have babies the minute high school or college was in their dust. Today's moms are independent girls who lived it up in their post-school chapters, learning what life was really all about: they were late-sleeping graduates, driven career makers, product junkies, fashion plates, travel mongers, and wellness freaks. And then they decided to take on a lucky hubby and have kids, but they knew they'd never leave the good life far behind. They suppose they're the first moms who get that bouncing babies doesn't mean bye-bye to everything that matters to them. Not only are they not giving it up, but they're also itching to share it all with their new little loves and pass these superb ideals down to the next liberated generation.

Rising above preconceived notions of a mother's look, her purpose, and her behavior, the Posh Mom is nothing like any who have come before her. She naturally lives by what we call the Posh Mom mottos, and when her days are dogged, she whispers them aloud to remind herself to continue to embrace her life, cherish her children, and treasure her guy. If you've already mastered them, our plaid Burberry (or very good look-alike) hats off to you. For the other 99 percent, aspire to these...

Posh Mom Mottos

1. Live for your kids.
2. Put family first...
3. ...and yourself on your to-do list.
4. Be hip, savvy, and sensational.
5. Embody confidence and humility.
6. Revel in the everyday.
7. Treat yourself to the fine things in life.
8. Epitomize style.
9. Make home your haven.
10. Treasure your friends.
11. Be a gracious hostess.
12. Get cultured, not pompous.
13. Know your etiquette.
14. Speak your mind.
15. Show grace under pressure.

This posh ideology feeds posh confidence. If you're not tuned in yet, you can be. You need only the craving, and to be ready for some impressive changes in your life.

Who Are We?

How do we know the Posh Mom so well? Silly, we *are* Posh Moms. Our sisters are chock full of posh. Our friends are, too. We are all out there living the Posh Mom life—on all kinds of budgets, in all kinds of places, in all kinds of ways.

Between us, we have done the pregnancy/morning sickness/too round to find a comfy position to sleep in thing five times (Amy has three children and Jara has two), suffered through that same number of labors, written umpteenth thank-you's for birth gifts, attended countless Mommy and Me classes, enrolled in years of preschools, and successfully transitioned to the uncharted world of elementary school. In addition, we've changed the closets over for the seasons and sizes more than one hundred times, invested in an array of balls (soft plush, Disney princess, Scooby-Doo, baseball, softball, soccer, football, tennis), and cheered on the sidelines of backyards, courts, and fields all over town. We've issued tear-infused time-outs or wimped out and "let this one slide." We've wiped innumerable tushies, including those belonging to our children's playmates.

But busy as we are, we didn't lose the battle for "me time" in the midst of all the mommy time. We couldn't. As much as we live for our families (see mottos #1 and #2 on page 8), we knew we'd be in a better place if we remembered to stay in touch with what made us who we were pre-kids. As moms and friends, and armed with a keen sense of inner self and outer style, we realized we were becoming the source and role model for other moms trying to get a grasp on how to pull off embracing motherhood while maintaining our fab womanhood. It became glaringly clear that until now, *posh* and *mom* were two words never uttered together, and we knew they deserved to be paired. But there was not a single book for moms to turn to for posh advice, ideas, inspiration, answers, or solidarity. (We know, we've looked.) So was born the idea of Posh Mom and the book we knew we had to write for her. In *Living the Posh Mom Life*, we give you the scoop on the Posh Mom talents and techniques, an inkling of what she loves, dislikes, would absolutely always do, and would never ever even think of. So, read on to get to know her. We're sure you'll want to corner her for a girl's night out.

After all, the Posh Mom is a sophisticated and dis-criminating parent who doesn't do books on child-rearing 101. Instead, she wants info that's stepped up a notch, info that's meant for a busy lady who's not just picking up her kids—and picking up after them. She wants to know how to juggle lunch dates and play dates, commuting and carpooling, me-time and mommy-and-me-time—and how to do with style, smarts, charm, and seemingly without effort. Because while she makes the time to make the effort, the PM doesn't always have tons of time, and she has to know how to work it and make it work, whether that means putting on the noodles and butter at home, volunteering to work her magic at the ticket booth at the school carnival, or getting gorgeous for couples' night out.

What's Inside

On these pages you'll find the inside info on the Posh Mom movement, what it means to be a Posh Mom (from your long sleek layers and your Converse all-stars to your naturally nurturing side and instinct that "me time" still matters), how you can reach your posh potential (whether you already possess a bit of posh or are starting from scratch and need a path mapped out), and what it will get you—that is, a new lease on a more souped-up model of your life.

We begin with a quiz to gauge your current posh status, suggestions on how to track your journey, and info to get you inspired. Then we divulge our findings on inner posh, and we give you that all-important permission to take time to treat yourself right and put yourself on your to do list (one of our Posh Mom mottos). We'll define a Posh Mom's many relationships—which ones she holds sacred, which ones she could do without (but has to live with anyway), and how she makes sure to give all the people in her life exactly what she expects in return. We also get down and dirty with outer posh, where we share tons of tips, beauty tricks, and closet must-haves. We explain how a PM makes her home comfortable yet beautiful to please all occupants and visitors. And a PM still fancies herself a party girl, with soirees for family and friends ranking high for satiating her fun side—so we'll bring to light all the dos and don'ts of posh entertaining. Then we take her out of the home to work or at least behind the closed doors of her home office, where the working Poshie balances the best of both worlds.

> Making the decision to have a child is momentous. It is to decide forever to have your heart go walking around outside your body.
> —Elizabeth Stone

And check out our Poshmom.com Picks sprinkled throughout these pages. They're must-haves, of-the-moments, and splurges that a fabulous mom like you craves and deserves. Picks make a cool mom's life that much more heavenly. And if you're pining for more, log on to poshmom.com and sign up for free indispensable bits of info for you and your hip offspring, delivered straight to your inbox—it doesn't get easier than that.

We hope you'll take all the tips, advice, and kinship this book serves up and infuse as little or as much as you want into your everyday life. Use it to remind yourself of all your fabulous qualities, even if they got hidden and buried under perpetual piles of laundry. When you've breezed through the book, do yourself a favor and keep it nearby, giving you strength to surpass all obstacles that motherhood places in front of you—like feeling drained due to repeating "brush your teeth" ten times, because of the dozen late-night phone calls to organize last-minute carpool changes, or the wayward caboose you trip over (that didn't get cleaned up) on your way to the bookshelf. We hope it will become your guide and your haven of inspiration and information that will motivate you beyond your most exquisite imagination. So come in and meet the Posh Mom (over a cup of coffee, perhaps?), celebrate her, and serve up camaraderie with other PMs. This book is also to encourage moms not yet in the scene to discover, develop, and delight in their poshness—everyone's got posh potential.

Chapter One

Getting Started

Here we go again. It's the first day of preschool and the brigade of SUVs files into the parking lot—some drivers early enough for a morning gab session, others right on time, and still more stragglers who are way late but don't even have an excuse since they don't look like they did anything for themselves in those minutes, including applying a basic coat of lip gloss.

Moms and tots pour out, and hugs and air-kisses fly around, even for and from all those "good friends" who didn't phone each other all summer. Taylor waits a beat before she steps out and surveys the situation, and then her own. Hair is looking extra sleek, the tee she's sporting is flattering her sun-kissed complexion (most from the fake stuff—she's addicted to SPF), and the Fiji pink polish tells all who peek at her pedicure that she is not giving up on summer yet. Yup, now she's happy she obeyed the alarm buzzing that pierced her early morning dreams, nudging her to get ready before she had to get the kids ready.

She smiles big at her little love safely buckled in her pony-covered seat (never too early to be instilling style), and her heart does a pitter patter that blows away any rush she ever felt from the private sample sale invites she was privy to pre-kids—Prada or not. The dimpled grin that comes back at her is the polar opposite of the fit-throwing frown her daughter sported just twenty minutes before, caused by a discussion of no flip-flops on the playground due to the sharp nature of wood chips. To her posh credit, Taylor counted to ten, shimmied the closed-toe shoe on (no, there was no shoving), made it to the car with plenty of time to drive without breaking the speed limit (too badly), and most importantly managed to have a scream-free ride, on her part, that is.

With a soft little hand (attached to a way cutely clad little bod) tucked into hers, she braves the rough crowd. Between the tragically messy, didn't-tend-to-myself-at-all-this-morning pony tails and I-just-threw-on-whatever-was-closest workout combos, she (thank gawd) spots a few members of her posse. Equally done but not overdone, they give each other knowing you're-looking-ca-yoote eyebrow arches or I-spied-those-capris-on-the-racks-and-they-look-awesome-on-you winks. Taylor spots a couple of new bags draped over their shoulders that she must cross off her shopping list, 'cause she would never do the copy-cat thing, especially on an item as key as a bag.

As she easily joins her crowd, throwing countless waves and "hi-right-back-at-yous" to acquaintances (posh and not), her daughter visits with her friends just a step away. Taylor dishes quickly because she has places to be: a coffee date with a friend whose last kid graduated from pre-school, a few minutes to check-in with her Blackberry (working part-time gives her the best of both worlds), then a fund-raising committee meeting that should end right before she has to tune back in to her kid's tunes as her dictatorial deejay is strapped back into the backseat.

She's psyched that the forced face time with friends is kicking up again and almost forgets her purpose until she hears a distant, "I wanna go play with my teachers and see my classroom!" She realizes it's her confident cupcake who can't wait to get inside, and she bids a hasty but ever sweet, "Talk to you later." This is not a mom who would say "one second" to her child so she can spend one more second jabbering with a friend, but rather one who thinks that un-posh behavior is downright disgraceful. And the day beats on....

Never underestimate the power of posh. When you're working it, you feel good, think cool, have a blast, love tenderly, laugh out loud, and look your ultimate. It can be all good most of the time, if you've got it. Want it? Here's how to get it: Just go for it! But first, you need to figure out where your starting block is. You don't want to bum rush your maintenance or makeover—you'll stumble and possibly snowball into a nasty embarrassing fall that will set you back weeks or more in your training. You know what we're talking about—like the time you were horrified to find you overdid it in a boob-baring shirt and high heels for a casual girls' night out. Once you know where you stand and how much work you need to put in, you'll know just how to set the pace for your saunter across the finish line—or the climb to your posh pinnacle.

Where Do You Stand?

Maybe you were the hip single girl who never thought she'd lose it—but "it" slipped away when maternity clothes and suburbia overtook your world. Or maybe you're trying so desperately to hold on to the life you led before kids that you're laying it on too thick and spreading yourself too thin. Or perhaps you're right on track, and you would just like to hear about others in their posh prime. Whatever your status, you obviously had the goods if you had the smarts to pick up this book. And, at some level, you've left your selfish part somewhat behind when you ran smack into the altruism of parenthood. But a Posh Mom doesn't have to let go all that matters. Sure, there are some peripheral NM (that is, non-mom) niceties that will suffer and that may even go by the wayside, such as taking half an hour to blow-dry every morning. But you were growing tired of that anyhow (or your arms were, right?) The Posh Mom has a willingness to say toodaloo to some of the outdated or old rituals or things for some new, amazing things in store. But a PM's everyday purpose and productivity remains the same as when she was without kids, even if there is a new driving force behind it (strapped into a five-point harness).

Her first day, week, even month home from the hospital (no matter what number child she's on) may have a PM second-guessing her posh status. In the melee of diapers, 3 a.m. feedings, pediatrician appointments, and plain old getting out of the house for a car ride with all the necessary gear, there doesn't seem to be much time for anything else.

Certainly a PM is entitled to be down for a count or two, but you know she doesn't fancy the position at all. Is she able to rally? If so, is it thanks to her guy, her friends, and her fab baby-sitter (if she's lucky enough)? Or was it due to her own superior, more-powerful-than-a-locomotive resilience? Or maybe she needs more time and more steps to finish the program—so that eventually, her grace, elegance, and groove picks up right where she left it under the blanket in the bassinet, enabling her to form sentences, return congratulatory

> I wanted to understand how I was going to go about finding true and lasting happiness in my life and how I was going to teach that to my daughter.
> —Madonna

phone calls, and write a stream of thank-yous, even to her husband's cousin Delia for the obviously re-gifted baby blanket (the previously filled-out tag hanging from the bag gave her up).

Before you reach your posh plateau (which will be different for every mom), you've got to grasp just how much posh you've got stashed deep down. Don't worry, we're not sending you off to discover that on your own. Take this quiz, tally your posh factor, and then you'll be good to get started, whether that means preparing to be the best Posh Mom you can be or preserving the goods you've already got.

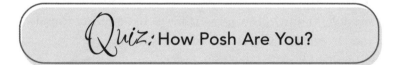

Quiz: How Posh Are You?

1. It's just post-bedtime story. No one is calling "I'm thirsty," hubby's doing dinner with the guys, and you're amazingly enough not near ready to crash. Now what?

   a. A delish bubble bath, a brain-candy "novel," then a catch-up phone chat with your best Poshie.
   b. Make lunches for tomorrow, then hit the sack yourself. It's all going to start again in the wee hours of the morning and you'll need your energy.

   c. Get a head start dialing your nightly round of gossip calls to friends.

2. Major sales are happening at the stores in town. What does that mean to you?

   a. Hightailing it there. You've had half a season of denim-envy, squinting to make out the labels attached to other women's stitched back pockets—it's your last chance to copy them.

   b. Nada. You've already done your shopping for the season.

   c. A definite addition to your date book, no matter how packed your day. More gear in everyone's closet and more moolah left over for must-have splurges.

3. Crazy day already—and it's only 6:45 a.m. You can only spare a quickie shower and no time to coif. What's your hair plan?

   a. Air-dry on the go—without a second thought to the frizz that will ensue.

   b. Tuck it cutely under a baseball cap you found on hubby's rack.

   c. A dollop of product and a takes-a-second-to-do sleek but chic pony.

4. You're at the supermarket with your three little peeps, ages 7, 5, and 3, when the perfect outing is zapped by your oldest, who insists she must have that neon-colored-made-from-ultra-fake-stuff-nothing-nutritious-about-it snack that you couldn't imagine anyone producing for consumption, let alone finding its way to your princess's stomach. As she digs in her pink Pumas and you stand firm in your own mules, you:

   a. watch her adolescent attitude hit an all-time high, then quickly give in to quickly quiet her down.
   b. let her hissy play out, then, ignoring any nosy passersby who seem to have nothing better on the agenda, tell her why you're not keen on the choice and that when she's ready to be reasonable, she can choose something else.
   c. grunt at her through gritted teeth, completely lose your calm, and stomp out of the store (dragging your three kids by the arms). No kid of yours will ever embarrass you like that, ever.

5. A friend, but not one on your "best" list, is dealing with a mini dilemma with possible major consequences. You:

   a. knock wood three times, thanking your lucky stars that the black cloud is not hovering over your white picket fence.

     b. are sad for her but you're not crying—rather you're the town crier disseminating all you know to everyone you know.

     c. give her space, then give her a day and a call to empathize. Offer to do what you can, even if it's just subbing for her carpool duty.

6. Who do you feel a Hollywood mommy connection with?

     a. Courteney Cox
     b. Brooke Shields
     c. Denise Richards

7. Your address book is chock full of friends:

     a. only with kids—your world revolves around them. Those without see you as strange and vice versa.

     b. old and new—you vow to keep ties with your pre-kid set but have made room for a select few mommy pals.

     c. by the hundreds. The more (and the more connected) the better, you say.

8. You and your posh posse are lunching to celebrate a BFF's b-day. When the idle chitchat turns to down-and-dirty gossip, you:

a. start slinging the mud, it's way too much fun to resist.
b. as a self-appointed mother hen, give your expert opinion on the subject. You have spoken, hear you roar.
c. pass on the cattiness—take the high road (even though it's almost too tempting).

9. Dinnertime at your house is sit-down and together-time. When the phone jingles with your neighbor ready to dish details about tomorrow's tennis game, you:

a. tell your kids, "just a sec," then gab for a minute or two.
b. don't give the ringing a second thought—there's no getting between you and moments with your loved ones.
c. check the caller ID in case of emergency, then let it go to voice mail—you'll call back.

10. For your kid's next birthday, plans include:

a. not much—just a few friends, a few games, and cake, of course.
b. calls to the hottest venues around to book time, (especially if tons of your friends' tots have already partied there).
c. a theme that's all about your little one's likes without going totally all out. Less is more, you always say.

Score

1.	a. 3	b. 1	c. 2	6.	a. 3	b. 1	c. 2
2.	a. 2	b. 1	c. 3	7.	a. 1	b. 3	c. 2
3.	a. 1	b. 2	c. 3	8.	a. 2	b. 1	c. 3
4.	a. 1	b. 3	c. 2	9.	a. 2	b. 1	c. 3
5.	a. 1	b. 2	c. 3	10.	a. 1	b. 2	c. 3

10 – 16 ● ● ●

Pre-natal Posh

You're definitely a mom who's all about her kids. You seem to live and breathe for them. Don't get us wrong, we do too, and we think it's a must-have Posh Mom quality—but so is recollecting that you've also got a life and you're in the prime of it. Whether it's hanging with friends, volunteering, working, or just stealing a few secs to catch up on the world (ask a friend without kids to fill you in—oh, that's right, you don't have any), it's vital you focus on the "m" word—not "mommy" but "me." Doing so is far from a luxury, it's an absolute necessity that will actually make you a hotter, hipper parent.

Don't think that your kids will feel abandoned—they'll not only still love you, they'll be proud of you and think you're a whole lot more fun—and you'll be proud of yourself too.

And when you've got more going on for yourself than well-visits to the pediatrician and the germs your kids picked up there, you'll dazzle the dinner party crowd filled with NMs and NDs (non-dads) by being able to jump right into a discussion about a just-released, award-winning film documentary. You might even be a whole new kind of sexy to your husband by putting the kids mostly out of mind when you put them to bed and cozy up to him in yours.

A Posh Mom gets that she's got to be at least minimally primped before heading out the door—clearly you're not yet heading in that direction. Regardless of the time left to get done up after rallying the kid troops each morning, you've got to make do and make something out of your 'do, not to mention paying a bit of attention to your outfit, too. Don't go for red carpet style, but do go for presentable at the a.m. drop-off wave. That means learning to groom your locks in a quick but cute style even when they give you sass. It also requires some mix-and-match of-the-moment closet staples that make the what-to-wear scenario a no-brainer. (Like tiny tees and the latest jeans—you can't go wrong and you'll look oh-so-right oh-so-early in the morning.)

You've got your work cut out for you—but you're off to a stellar start. After all, "live for your kids" is our number one Posh Mom motto. Now you've just got to get through mottos 2–15. Remember that while kids are essential to a Posh Mom's existence and are responsible for her eternal bliss, they don't completely define her. She's got lots to round it out: her man, good friends, fab style, and, of course, an amazing sense of self in all she says and does.

17 – 23 ● ● •

Think You're Posh but You're Not

Easy, rough rider. You want so badly to be fabulous it hurts—you and everyone around you who has to watch. No worries. We're here to help, starting by reining you in. Remember that being a PM is not about putting up appearances or proving that you're posh. It's about thinking it for yourself then letting it work its way out naturally.

It's understandable that you want to be in the know, but you don't have to let everybody know when you are. That's the difference: A PM knows she gets it and that's good enough for her. Listen, why make chain phone calls so you can be the news bearer on the "is it a muffin top or is it her first trimester" status of an acquaintance three-times removed, when you could have saved up your energy to get busy with your hubby when he got home?

To you, being tapped in means having your tentacles in every social circle you can. You'd rather be exposed to the masses rather than tucked into a private corner table with one or two true pals. You might be staking your social claim, but your kids are not always the beneficiaries. They seem more of an accessory you can cast off (to the baby-sitter, at a playdate, with your parents) when your social agenda needs attention. Maybe you're scared to be unavailable to the social set who counted on you for advice, friendship, and fun pre-kids, and you want to have lots of entry space in your PDA for all the new moms with little ones. Go ahead, freshen your mani for a girls' night out, you deserve it. After all, a PM indulges in kissing the kids good-bye for a time. But don't forget that she does not employ the kiss-off on a regular basis. And there are certain moments (meal times, bedtime, bath time) that are absolute quality time in which she doesn't let anything interfere. Remember that you have a fabulous family at home who want to dine with you (even if dinner came from a macaroni box) and go drinking (water spiked with O. J.) and hang out all night (books, videos, lullabies, and their attempts to pass out in your bed). And you don't even need to be slotted into their calendar.

When not at home, sometimes it's okay to let a fit play out (as long as it's not so over the top that it will cause the store you're in to start losing clientele), and it's your job as mom to retain complete composure. Yelling, dragging, and under-the-breath expletives are totally uncalled for and completely tacky—not at all indicative of a Posh Mom's demeanor.

When dealing with others, your posh radar is set to ultra-sensitive frequency. You know just where all the town Poshies send their kids to classes, what jeans brand they favor now, what houses they're moving into, and where they travel over the winter and during the summer. And if you can't join them (shop the shop, walk the walk, vacation in the Caribbean), you tell the news to anyone and everyone. Stop it. Every PM thinks for herself. Not every piece of clothing has to be a designer original, but your thoughts and ideas certainly do. And remember, you're setting an example for your kids, who think you spew the gospel. It's your duty to pass posh on to them—the real thing, not the wannabe.

24 – 30 ● ● ●

Posh Present and Accounted For
You still got it, baby. You're just as hip and utterly amazing as you were before you got the word you were cooking up a mini posh package. You didn't lose yourself, you just expanded your horizons (and your belly), because being a mom was going to be just as grand as any single or married-without-children life you were leaving behind.

You walk into a room and people notice, but you probably don't even notice they do. Your grace and style are the epitome of posh. You love fashion, live for products and appreciate all they can do, couldn't do without your friends, and treasure your family. Your parenting techniques come so naturally that Oprah's people should be booking you as a guest to share the wealth. But you know it's not as easy as some may think. Sometimes even you don't know where your patience reserve comes from, like the time when you kept composed after the juice box spurted all over the leather seats in the car whose odometer hadn't even reached triple digits.

You had kids when the time was right (or when the pregnancy stick finally read positive), and you appreciate every minute of every day with them. You treat being a mom as the most serious and important position ever, one that even puts the kibosh on other happenings in your life. But you know not to turn down every invite out that doesn't involve the little peeps, since you deem "me time" away from mommy time as *tres* important. No doubt you get guilt in your gut when you kiss their cutie faces good-bye, but you know they'll be just fine (you employ the best baby-sitter out there or are lucky enough to have Grandma close by) and that they'll benefit from a refreshed you.

Your goals are set to earth's reality meter, and you never expect you'll be posh all day, every day—and you don't try. Bad days happen—and when they do, you kick in to automatic mode for today, and plan to start anew tomorrow. Then you plug into your support network. You'll phone your sister or one of your trusted BFFs to vent so you don't take your sour state out on your kids. But most of your days you make good ones. You're not feigning June Cleaver, but you're shooting to make it as good as it gets—for yourself and your family.

Moving Forward

Trust us. We get that your days are so jam packed with driving your little Miss and Mr. Daisies, making lunch, working, planning dinner, managing the house, minding your marriage, attempting to keep a social life, and, oh yes, scheduling *your* personal to-dos, that there's not time left to put anything else heady on the agenda. Well, make room for this. You'll be glad you did. No plane ticket or full tank of gas necessary to embark on an amazing journey to track down your hip and happening inner self. With it in your sights, you turn inside out so you can start revealing (and then dressing the part for) what you're really made of.

You've already taken the very first step: hunkering down to get the lowdown. You answered the questions (a Posh Mom knows she needs to count on herself, so make sure you've answered each question with enduring honesty), then sat through a pretty good dishing about what's posh about you and what's not. Kudos. It's hard for a girl to look in the mirror (except when it's the skinny dressing room variety) and listen to someone else dress her up

> Mothers are the most instinctive philosophers.
> —Harriet Beecher Stowe

and down. But we said what we said because Poshies tell the truth to comrades—and the advice and info we dispense as a result will be as valuable as any you get from a dear old friend, one hundred percent for your best.

So be prepared to do some soul searching before you go searching for the perfect jeans. Anyone can have the sense to match up Prada belts and shoes, but that doesn't mean she has the sensitivity to know that her good friend is stressed about an upcoming MRI (most likely nada) even though she insists she's not. Blessed with good sense as well as good style, a Posh Mom is the well-rounded mom and woman. The Posh Mom Mottos on page 8 are what she drives toward—and are where PMs in the making and on a maintenance schedule need to begin.

Words to Live By: The Posh Mom Mottos

Because of her independent nature, a PM would never subject herself to others' rules of thought. It is perfectly acceptable for her, however, to be in agreement or inspired by those ideas that are particularly well-crafted (modest, aren't we?). So think of the Posh Mom mottos as guides. Individually they are not new news, but together they are a front page story. Read through them, picture yourself partaking, and most important, don't write off any that don't do it for you (a PM never passes judgment). Some of these mottos are aspirations you may deem foreign now, but soon enough they will become second nature. For example, if number 6, "Revel in the everyday" seems like too much work, just make it work for you. On those days when your only view of the kids is in the rearview mirror, where you can see them either experimenting with different ways to buckle while karate starts in five (and sensei gives looks that say "karate chop" to late arrivals) or fighting over the last piece of Double Bubble before one of their other thousand activities, revel in that. Treasure the beautiful, sweet faces—sticky gum mustache, whining, and all. Even though you can't fathom it now, as every older mom who coos at your baby while you're strollering through the Gap tells you, it goes by so bleeping fast.

Write down the mottos on the first page of a fabulous book or journal (ooh, do we feel a shopping trip coming on?). Find one in your favorite color or in a print that charms your vintage capris off. It can have lined pages (for those neat and neurotic Poshies) or blank slates (some PMs do their best thinking when freewheeling). And get a pen just for this purpose too—one that is off-limits to sticky, pudgy little fingers who like to doodle with anything within reach and will carry it off to toy boxes unknown. Humor us here—even if your preference veers more toward the PDA technique, for this exercise it's necessary to break out penmanship and be in technology-free sync with your thoughts.

Make a cup of cocoa or a hot cup of tea, or have that refreshing glass of soda you've been craving but trying to keep far from your little one's taste buds. Curl up on a favorite chair or perch on the pillows you painstakingly picked out for your bedroom but never seem to be around long enough to lounge on, and have some good old-fashioned "me time" (we knew you could do it).

Your first assignment: Study the mottos. Decide which seem most imminently attainable, including those ideals that may already be ingrained in your every day. Is it true that you tell your kids you love them a hundred times a day, and that you hug them whenever you get a chance (or they let you)? Go girl, onto the next.

A PM juggles any number of these at various times during the day, and you should strive to do the same. Surely a girl can't always put herself on the to-do list, especially when she's putting kids and family first. But Poshie is guilt-free after a day of playing princess and ponies (on her hands and knees and with a saddle on her back), and she doesn't think twice about planning "early to bed" night for the kids—leaving her extra time for online shopping, magazine perusing, or catching up on TiVo. And she sets goals, always reaching higher, whether in the boardroom or the exercise room. This motto thing is no different. Start with one, two, or five mottos a day that you think you can hit. Shoot for seven, then ten, and more. (Hint: For instant gratification— something every PM loves—make one of your must-hit mottos "put yourself on your to-do list." If you're keeping a journal, you're doing just that!)

Work your book like you know you can work a room, in whatever fashion works for you. Make each page about one motto. Or assign each page a day and give your chosen mottos space there. Then recap at the end of the day or the week—whenever and wherever you can find some quiet, private time to write and reflect. (It might be best for you to pick a night of the week for this task and stick to it—maybe one night the kids are spent from a day packed with activities and will likely crash early.) Then crack open the journal and start putting your pretty pen to paper, charting your posh progress.

This exercise is more than patting yourself on the back (although with all the points you're racking up, that action might burn some unwanted calories). A PM is always clued in to what's remarkable—and not—about herself. She walks around with the mottos naturally ingrained in the forefront of her mind—right behind her side-swept bangs—and you should too, eventually. For now, writing it all down will get you dancing to the resulting beat of it and keep you on your soft, just-pumiced toes in the future. Like when you say sayonara to that fourth lunch date for the week and choose instead to pick your daughter up from school (saving her the long, sweaty bus ride home) and then take her out for ice cream. Or when you're about to pop into a meeting at work and you call home to tell the kids you love them instead of taking one last look through your notes. Do either of these, and you've "lived for your kids." When you see a sale sign and sail in, when you count to ten when you really wanted to raise a completely monster-mom voice at your little terrors, or when you dashed into a bookstore to buy the latest best seller for bath time (yours)—all qualify as reaching the mottos and are fodder for your written words.

But don't just spill all the good stuff you're up to. Any Posh Mom knows she's got to face the bad stuff head on if she's going to beat it, just like a bully on the playground needs confrontation. Let's say you were idly gossiping about a chickie in town (who has tried to hone in on your best friendship a little too backhandedly), or maybe you said a few choice words to the guy in the pickup who cut you off while your children looked at you wide-eyed from the backseat. Sometimes seeing "your bads" in black and white makes you face facts and realize you never want to own that horrid behavior again.

Get Inspired

A Posh Mom's finely tuned radar (poshdar, if you will) allows her to pick up all that's fabulous from people around her. From those tidbits she may be tempted to glean what she likes and what she doesn't, what makes her feel good and what doesn't, what she'd like to emulate and what she wouldn't. And rightly so, it's called inspiration, and a Posh Mom in the making needs to draw on it. Start with the obvious: Magazines, favorite celebrities, characters from movies or books. All are a wealth of information that you can apply to all parts of your everyday, from style, to beauty regimens, to family togetherness, food choices, kids' names, and more.

Then look to other places closer to home: friends, relatives, people you pass in the market or see in the park. Is there anything about them that strikes you as hitting the mark? Use that "she's got it" feeling as your I-can-be-like-her motivation. After all, you want to admire yourself (and have others do the same), too. You know what we're talking about: when you're on the phone with your sister, both sets of kids screaming in the background, and she excuses herself to speak in calm but still strong tones. Your jaw is dropping to the hardwood floor cause her little speech worked, so you give it a try and are astonished that it works in your house, too—and now there's no sending your brood fleeing from the room in fear of losing story privileges that night.

Buddy Up

As much as a PM likes her alone time, she also values the companionship of good friends. So don't set off on this ride alone. Enlist the help of a pal you can count on, be completely honest with, and are totally comfortable talking to. After all, you will be divulging your imperfections (few and far between that they are). It would help if she also aspires to be posh, even if she doesn't know it yet. Or better yet, if she's your icon, ride the coattails of her already established Posh Momness. Either way, it might be your sister, your oldest friend, or the newest one you clicked with when you moved to town. It should just be someone you trust with your life—okay, just your lifestyle, but it's still ultra important. It's imperative you hold her opinions in high regard and she should feel the same about yours. A PM values friends who are good listeners and who won't put on a pout if she's truthful (never cruel)—and a Posh Mom would only give the same in return. Your posh partner needs to be someone who can tell you (without you minding) that the hair you thought looked so cute in the same updo you sport to sleep in (since college) is just not happening when you're out and about—or that your husband's jean jacket from the eighties (you've had it since you were former high school sweethearts) was cool then—lumberjack flannel lining and all—but is so not now, so stop wearing it. And you should feel you can do the same for her. She's also the one to call and say, "What do you mean you're not going for girls' night out? Get your buttocks in gear—I'm picking you up in half an hour."

And when you get there, don't feel like you need to strut your stuff at a cranked-up volume—whether that's your rekindled interest in geology or your newly purchased underpinnings. You're just going to be good company 'cause you're starting to think by the seat of your own derriere-lifting jeans—not just by the ones filled with your little one's droopy diaper. Use your journal as ammo when you find yourself falling into the familiar and easy (but boring by now) conversations about preschool and play-dates. Talk up the premiere of a TV show you watched, the riveting book you just read (imagine), or the hottie trainer who just started working at your gym. There's also pleasure in listening with wide opened (and undisturbed) ears to the forays of your friends, as you sit back and sip a cocktail. Cheers!

Anatomy of a Posh Mom

No matter the duds she's donning, these are the innate attributes a Posh Mom wears morning, noon, and night. Check out this checklist like you would another Poshie, from head to toe—this is the picture of posh:

Head (can't see this one, but trust us, it's there)
Chock full of confidence
Aspires to be fabulous, not perfect

Heart
Nurturing, loyal, and sometimes worn on her sleeve

Hair
Always done—never over-coiffed (even when time allows)

Eyebrows
Two distinct—and well-groomed—beings

Eyes
Enough mascara to make up for less than a full night's sleep

Nose
Boogie-free, even if her children's are not

Lips
Not so glossy as to prevent petite puckers

Breath
Never scary, even after a Starbucks pick-me-up

Earrings and Necklace
Gifts from her guy who saw her performance in the delivery room

Watch
Never without
Keeps her (relatively) on schedule for carpool or commuting

Nails
In a pale shade (best for concealing chips until she can squeeze in a manicure)

Bag
Sensational, of the moment, a big splurge, and big enough for her and her kids' essentials

Jeans
The perfect fit and dark-washed to hide tiny finger-prints

Legs
Covered due to lack of shower shave time

Thongs
No VPL—ever

Shoes
Stylish yet not too runway as to cause blisters when carting children and large shopping bags

Fragrance (at wrist and neck)
And an extra spritz on her hair when there's no time to wash

Child
Her ultimate and most precious accessory

Chapter Two

Inner Posh

T he voice mail went around to the entire Posh posse. "12:00, Splash Restaurant, to celebrate Taylor's thirty-fifth." And at noon, Taylor and five friends arrive at the scene (and to-be-seen-at establishment). These six fabulous warrior women of the zany morning rush came through the battle mentally frenzied but stylishly unscathed. Kids seen off at the bus stop, ingredients for tonight's shrimp and veggie skewers picked up, mommy-and-me music attended. Don't forget to throw in a workout, a shower (it counts even though they didn't stay long enough to steam up the glass), and a list of completed phone calls, including one to the office and one to the Saturday night baby-sitter (a must for end-of-the-week sigh of relief).

Cheek pecks and big hugs saying, "been there, done that much too, comrade, now it's girl time" go around the table. When the waiter approaches, this groovy group is so busy exchanging kudos about new purchases and newly buffed complexions, riding a high of adult convo, they barely hear him ask, "Can I get you young ladies something to drink?" The "young" reference makes perfect sense. Their chic hair, well-toned triceps in tiny tees, and sleek cell phones that go table-top pronto (you'd think they were waiting for a boyfriend's call when reality is they are on call for kids) don't belong to a bunch of traditional matriarchs. They belong to these modern moms who are anything but conventional.

There's a break in the banter long enough to order—they each get their own souped-up salad entrée and a few fancy appetizers for the table to share, like best girlfriends do. Then the talk turns spicier than the blackened Chilean sea bass on the menu. "That girl Andrea is a slut," slips Jill. The worst possible trait a married woman with children can possess, agrees the Posh roundtable (aside from curled-under bangs left over from the eighties). Her flirtatiousness with other married men pales in comparison to last weekend's incident, in which she kissed a stranger at the bar (yes, it's true) while her husband was seated at a table close by. Today's lunch attendees have become judge and jury of the scandalous event.

As birthday girl, Taylor is given the Posh podium first. There is no love lost between Taylor and Andrea—truth be known she has batted her eyes at Taylor's husband more than once, and although her appearance is less than threatening, that kind of behavior is never appreciated nor *should it be tolerated. Bashing Andrea is what the occasion calls for—the hussy has broken vows, for heaven's sake. But although it's easy for anyone to get caught up in a meow factor moment, there are subject matters much more worthy of discussing, and Taylor doesn't skip a beat in resetting the Posh tone. Her verdict. "I think I'll have the mango sorbet," is quickly (albeit a bit reluctantly) followed by five equally yummy dessert orders. Score one for Posh Moms taking the high road even when the low one could have been so totally fun.*

Having it all is a myth that got chucked out the Posh Mom's maternity ward window when she delivered her first pint-sized posh. Any mother who thinks she can still dote solely on herself seems more like an ogre (and not the sweet Shrek variety either) than a mom. But the selfless mom is every bit as dreadful an example to her kids (never shopping and lunching with friends does qualify as misery). Catering to your little one's needs *and* snagging time for yourself is the dreamy equilibrium every PM vows to strive for. After all, the

> When you are a mother, you are never really alone in your thoughts. A mother always has to think twice, once for herself and once for her child.
> —*Sophia Loren*

more you cultivate your inner posh, the more energy you'll have left for your petite ones.

Early morning ready time is one place a PM struts this kind of stuff. She knows just when to stop snoozing the alarm so she can dash into the shower before her entourage comes clamoring in. She can get the kids ready (making a breakfast that goes well beyond Pop-Tarts and Froot Loops and all the way to the stove) and spiff up herself, even if that means a low-slung ponytail, fabulously fitted jeans, and a swipe of gloss. With the big kids sent on the school bus and the little one dropped at preschool, she sets out for some solo time. The working Posh Mom takes busy to an unfathomable level, and needs to stake claim to alone time before the sun comes up or after it goes down (and the kids go down as well). Easy as that—or is it? Don't worry, you'll get there, too—whether you need to learn the basics, work on what you've got, or just brush off the dust and brush up.

Confidence

As an NM, the Posh Mom had a healthy dose of confidence. In no particular order, she was: riding a cool career wave, part of a tight-knit group of posh pals, hooked up with her Mr. Right, honing her hobbies, caring meticulously for herself, and looking fabulous and fine. Even so, she understood that the importance of really looking good meant she had to feel good, too—mind, body, and soul. And she did, without anybody lighting a match under her posh assets to do so.

She was perfectly at home in a crowd but never had a problem bowing out to spend some alone time with take out and the sofa, even if that meant taking a rain check for the hottest new club (although she would never leave a friend to fly solo if her friend begged her to accompany her). She was mindful of what made everything whole and right in her world: bubble baths, belting it out with the radio, long runs, pure chocolate, and never being too shy to indulge in any or all.

Many a posh gal's confidence was pumped up tenfold by the very thing that made her life even more remarkable—giving birth. You go, girl. In one magical moment, she brought life into this world and took on the awesome responsibility of helping it soar. Nothing as lofty as to perfection, but straight up to the best it can be, just like she leads her own life. A Posh Mom's self-assurance is bona fide, and the opposite of attitude. There's no strutting around with a sour puss or with her nose in the air. There's a name for that—bad behavior. A PM doesn't do it

> Motherhood brings as much joy as ever, but it still brings boredom, exhaustion, and sorrow, too. Nothing else ever will make you as happy or as sad, as proud or as tired, for nothing is quite as hard as helping a person develop his own individuality especially while you struggle to keep your own.
> —Marguerite Kelly and Elia Parsons

and sees right through it—it's nothing more than camouflage for an imposter. Her M. O. is way different. She's completely cool with who she is and would never go trying to prove she's something she's not— she has no desire and certainly lacks the time. No, a PM is authentic to the core.

Pumping up your ego to reach ultra posh status is no different than anything you've done in life up until now—it takes sweat equity. Your parents always preached "you don't get something for nothing" as well as "hard work pays off." It's not too late to take their advice. You know they were right (as we realized way back during college admissions when our safety school almost became our reach school!). A true Posh Mom doesn't behave like a child who stubbornly won't listen. Even if you fancy yourself a confident cookie, do not skip this chapter. Everyone needs a shot of self-assurance, even if it's just a booster.

Have you become the "bare minimom"? You know, the mother whose downturn started as soon as she changed her first poopy diaper. License to slack and then some. No more exercise to start the day right, ice cream as another food group, and Baby Einstein as the closest thing to learning she'll attempt. Her kids are like her American Express card: she's not leaving home without them so don't nobody try to schedule lunch at a restaurant with tablecloths! Then a good long look in the mirror reveals the mutated version of herself, and it scares the sweatpants off her. Unfit for public consumption, unfit period, and spirits squashed and withered. If you are like this mom, get over yourself girl, and start getting back into yourself, Poshie.

Or yours may be a different story. Maybe perfection has been your motto in your relationships, at work, with your wardrobe. Too-high expectations for your new status as parent go vamoose as soon as you are introduced to your howling, feeding, and sleeping-on-his-own-schedule baby. You see clearly (through blurry, sleep-deprived eyes) that your former modus operandi is not going to apply to this particular eighteen-year project, and the reality has you chasing your tail. It's that feeling of perpetual dizziness that's got you deflated. To top it off, maybe that self-assurance that took a lifetime to build got thrown away with the placenta, and you're pining to get it back.

> You have to love your children unselfishly. That's hard. But it's the only way.
> —*Barbara Bush*

No matter your telenovela, wake up tomorrow morning and get your pretty pedicure out of the gate to reclaim, seek, or revel in your confidence—it'll be an awesome journey, even if you take it in baby steps. Think about it: You just created a miracle. In comparison, re-creating the way you think is cake. Just follow the posh recipe, one ingredient at a time.

Posh Pick-Me-Ups

Start with the hormones (pregnancy, pre-menstrual, and every other variety—where were these hormones hiding when we were younger?). Add in the mild case of exhaustion due to middle-of-the-night potty calls (no longer booty calls, if in fact that was ever your calling). Toss in the total and utterly weighty responsibility for mini beings, and you have all your low-ego culprits in line. Blame your scraping-the-bottom animation on one or all—jump-starting your spirit is the first step to getting back your verve (and it has nothing to do with the scary cables in the trunk of your car!).

The Posh Mom's remedy: small, unabashedly self-involved, feel-good treats. Sure, a spa weekend is more than well-earned, but reality in the form of a squirt of yogurt from their squeeze-up tube hits her smack in her forehead as if to say, "You're not going anywhere." So she chooses to uplift with these little harmless things that make a swell mom shamelessly happy:

Chill Out ● ● •

This isn't news to you. Everyone around you is evangelizing your need to release a bit—and doing so in your face. But how can that be done when so much else needs to be done? Bottles need sterilizing, the kids' favorite new movie needs to be sought out on DVD, after-school tennis spaces need to be snapped up. It doesn't matter—you've got to case up lady, if only just for a moment. Try twenty minutes for Oprah (TiVo it to skip commercials) or a minimal ten minutes with your coffee. Or how about touching up your nails, and watching the top coat dry, reminding you that there is a "you"? The after-effects of these minor liberations are like a jolt of caffeine without the skipped heartbeat. You'll see: Even if you missed the last space in the four o'clock tennis clinic, you'll have the stamina to call around to find another.

Take a Whiff ● ● •

Sometimes improving your mood requires nothing more than a quick sniff of a scented candle labeled "Vitality." Other cases of the blues need more intensive aromatherapy: To ward off the weight of the fifty-two commitments in store today, break out a perfume that harkens back to carefree college days. And there's always a massage with aromatherapy oils and lots of deep breathing, perfect to wash away memories of the weekend's visit from your nosy sister-in-law who overstayed her welcome big-time.

Breathe in…

Tune In ● ● •

Piles of articles that we can't find time to read have been written about the power of music to cure a bad case of mope. Mommy moodiness (brought on by kids who ironically feel the brunt of it) is well-documented too, and the exact reason tunes should be playing from the car ride to school all the way through dinner preparation. It may be classical that calms you before the storm of the day, or maybe an eighties disco blast from the past that makes your minutes on the elliptical fly by. Either way, load the MP3 player and don't forget to turn it up.

Especially crank it up when you're alone—because when you've got backseat passengers, there's never a shortage of orders barked from pint-sized deejays: "it's too loud—your music is hurting my head," or "change the station," blatantly missing the "please" and regard for your taste in music. When that happens, try crossover tunes and jingles (see posh picks on the next page) that hit a rhapsodic chord in adults and kids alike. Somehow kids catch on to the easy lyrics, and Posh Moms can bear them even if they are not her first choice of listening material.

If all else fails, make sure the dictatorship reigns in the end, because if the

Poshmom.com Pick

iTRAIN has downloadable workouts for your iPod or MP3 player so you can sculpt, sweat, and stretch with instruction from big name Hollywood trainers. Plus, the background music will really get you moving. Much like you pump up your kids with encouragement to complete their tasks, this trainer in your earbud pushes you with "stay with it" and "you can do it."

chauffeur is forced to stomach *I'm a Little Teapot* past the fourth time, the teapot won't be the only thing "all steamed up"—mom will be letting off her own road rage, to the detriment of everyone's safety and happiness.

Sing Along ● ● •

As a single gal, did you aspire to be the next Paula Abdul, belting out a great "Straight Up" with your friends? Remember those days as you turn down the Kidz Bop and tune up your vocals. Singing is empowerment and can prevent you from crying it out. Take it from the shower (the best possible place to assure a solo performance) to nighttime tucking-in rituals, to possibly a stage at a party you throw your husband. A good rendition of "I Will Always Love You" will be as good for him as for your ego (especially when you're accompanied by a well-tuned karaoke backup).

Posh Picks: Top 10 Good Crossover Tunes

American Pie
> *Don McLean*

Sweet Home Alabama
> *Lynyrd Skynyrd*

Drift Away
> *Uncle Kracker*

The Gambler
> *Kenny Rogers*

Mandy
> *Barry Manilow*

Bananza (Belly Dancer)
> *Akon*

Hotel California
> *The Eagles*

Since You've Been Gone
> *Kelly Clarkson*

Hips Don't Lie
> *Shakira*

Cat's in the Cradle
> *Harry Chapin*

Take a Warm One ● ● •

Nothing helps a posh-impaired person revive like a bath. A shower is for cleanliness and so you don't start your day already running twenty-nine minutes behind. A tub, however, is for soothing away all that went wrong in your day. Replace the sparkly strawberry-flavored bubbles and protective spout cover with some relaxing bath salts and a row of fragrant candles to fence out any bad karma. Then submerge in the pool of warm water to create the illusion of a mini-spa that requires no previous appointments and no travel time. But just because there is no cancellation fee for no-shows, don't even think of skipping out on it.

The Joy of Shopping ● ● •

Stores, kiosks, gas station mini-marts, anyplace you can make a purchase brings on a smile—even the low-priced-but-never-lowly drugstore. The rush of discovering something new or sought after can take your mood from blah to blast-off in a quick cash register ka-ching. Whether you have the funds and are coming home with bags full of goods or you're on spending moratorium (after the receipt and discussion of last month's credit card statement), the simple act of entering a place of sale pacifies a Posh Mom who is easily satisfied—at least in this arena.

Search It Out ● ● •

Not your soul, but the web. A PM doesn't denounce the power of scoring late night purchases, virtually touring future travel destinations, and finding feel-good sites with bits of must-have info for you, the hip and savvy mom (www.poshmom.com!). But there's also a hidden source of camaraderie out there: the mommy message boards. What's more, everything's not happy go lucky on the Internet; there are some miserable moms lurking. Your keyboard is your most valuable source for spying on how atrociously other moms are handling their lives. As a Peeping Tara you'll find moms who hate themselves, detest their kids, and hope harm will find their husbands. You may not think it's appropriate to take pleasure in other people's low points, but it is anonymous, and it's a scene that will undoubtedly propel you to surpass the job they are doing. Message boards can do amazing things for erecting a strong foundation of a Posh Mom—and it can help you feel like a superstar. Learning that in comparison you are nowhere close to doing a hack job on yourself or your family can overwhelmingly beat down any lack of self-confidence you may have had.

Stolen Glances ● ● •

It seems like some women get confidence dripped through their epidural needle. Suddenly you find yourself envying the girl next door for her gung-ho mom spirit when she was nothing more as an NM than your uninspirational neighbor. Seeking answers to how she does it, you decide there's no harm in observing and maybe even taking a page from her posh playbook. Make a long playdate for the kids and stay to check out how she copes when the tough stuff rears its head: sharing their "special" toy, pleading for the fifth sugar snack, and the always sticky, "I don't want her to go home. I want to play forever!"

Attention! ● ● •

When a mom has great posture, she just reeks with authority (and it prevents her from one day becoming a hunched over posh grandmother). So stand up tall, throw your shoulders down and back, and use the extra power of the inch or two you gained in height to your advantage when vying for a parking spot, chastising the kids, or insisting to the dry cleaner that the unsightly spot wasn't on your pants when you brought them in.

Repeat After Me ● ● •

Mantras are helpful tools for awakening your inner self, and repeating them daily while washing clothes or dishes is a good way to remind yourself to see the sunny side of things. Try these:

For spirit—I vow to feed my inner self at least a little everyday. The little bit needs to be in addition to and not replaced by chocolate kisses and Oreos.

For body-—Treat my body as a temple, but one in which the occasional cocktail is allowed.

For mind—As sapped as my head is from having babies, it needs stimulation. The Wiggles are cute, but world news will resuscitate my brain.

For self—I breathe, therefore I am. And therefore I get to do for myself, even if I am last following what seems like an eternity of bedtime rituals for the kids.

For family—I will do and say what I need to and never be embarrassed to be a mom, even if that means repeated phone calls to school to make sure one small problem is solved.

For home—I will take pride in mi casa no matter how *pequeño* or *grande* it is. I will buy fresh flowers to take attention away from big laundry piles that need folding.

Posh Mom Q&A: Jara Gets Going

The situation
I feel like mom-o-rama this morning. Showered and looking fine, big kid off on the school bus (with time to spare for mascara and little love notes in the lunchbox) and baby strapped into the high chair eating and wearing mush. Everything is going according to plan: I'm combining my coffee with calmness (how often does that happen?) and brimming with confidence. Then the phone rings, and a new, possibly cool friend-with-baby wants me by her side for a strollercize—in fifteen minutes. I would like the exercise, but I hate the word "strollercize" and am paralyzed by the thought of the preparation in the puny moments I have to make it happen. This just wasn't on the to-do list. How will I fit in time to wipe down my food-covered little noodle, bundle her up, strap her in, collect toys for the stroller, pack the diaper bag full of any must-haves I can't anticipate (including cell phone if the school calls about your older one, and cookie bribes for your stroller occupant), and reapply lip gloss?

The solution:
I won't, partly because babies are high maintenance and partly because I am. So I ask my friend if she can

sit tight for a few extra *minutos* and say I'll be happy to stroll by her side a bit later. I channel my pre-phone call positive aura into successfully and calmly completing a routine I have gotten quite good at when the pressure's not on—getting out the door. It helps that I learned this lesson to the wise: It ain't like it used to be pre-kids, when I said "Money—check, keys—check, lipstick—check" and walked out the door. Knowing this, I packed away stuff last night (refill diaper and wipes, powdered formula portions, assigned-to-stroller-duty toys, a little tube of a rosy cheek gel to look alive) to help avoid the madness of gathering it quickly on the days I'm not the benefici-ary of a slower-motion allowance. This way I can grab and go rather than making backward strides in a whirlwind of chaos when all I want to do is fast-track it out the door—as I do today.

Work It Out

An office job could never demand the degree of task-management as a home filled with children can—no matter how high-powered the position may be. Luckily, forty-five minutes with a treadmill can do as much to clear the Posh Mom's head as a more costly session at the shrink—and she never doubts its power to put things in perspective. It's a Posh Mom's policy to exercise no matter how skinny Minnie she is at that moment. Exercise can extinguish a bad bout of PMS, keep your body perky and primed, and even provide enough endorphins to take you through preparation of multiple dinners for all your finicky eaters. Even short sessions plus a shower will have you feeling like a dynamic force to be reckoned with. Not much else (besides hallucinogens regulated by the Federal Drug Administration) can have that much of a catapulting effect on your mood.

Pound the Pavement Solo ● ● •

Something about you running alone against the wind can produce a surge of assuredness. Don't attempt calling a friend for a stroll and chat. Your results will probably amount to nothing—short of a good gabfest you might as well have shared over a Starbucks. No, you need alone time to think and to get that runner's high. The endorphins flow right into the part of your brain responsible for healthy cockiness, and your resulting svelte body can't hurt in the confidence department, either.

Kick It Up ● ● •

Flash back to *Flashdance* or even further. Leave the sweatbands and leg warmers behind, but do go for hip-hop, salsa, or tango class that will not only be good for your cardio but that will prevent you from falling prey to Elaine (BFF to Seinfeld)-type moves for your once-a-year trip to a club or second-wedding reception.

No Excuses ● ● •

How often (or not) you fit in those minutes (or hopefully, hours) depends on a number of factors. How much help do you have? Full-time baby-sitter, mother who lives within an hour's drive, a metro-sexual husband who can chat up moms at pick-up better than you? Don't think you're off the hook and off the Stairmaster if your answer is "none of the above." There's some friend out there in your same desperate situation for child care. She can play baby-sitter for yours while you burn treadmill rubber and anxiety, and you can return the favor the next day. Or stop cursing the advent of the jogging stroller just because it leaves you with no reason not to, and venture out with one. You can take the youngest ones who pre-school won't enroll for dual duty fresh air and a nap. Your mode of physical fitness comes down to your willingness to sweat or refusal to, and that will help you decide between Pilates or pile jumping.

Alternative Reasons ● ● •

A posh attitude doesn't have to be your only reason to strap on the spandex: there's a plethora of ulterior motives to prod you to move your body. Are you looking to fit into your pre-pregnancy jeans or simply looking to get fit to run after those who carry your genes? Did you promise yourself you'd do a big project in the next year that didn't have anything to do with crayons? It may be that training and running in a marathon (notice we didn't say "completing") will pump you up mentally and physically. Take a look at your goals and see what exercise might solve...

Upwardly Mobile ● ● •

Help yourself and your ego by rounding up all numbers that will make you feel better if they're bigger, such as pounds lost (i.e., seven and a half goes to ten), minutes you completed on any machine at the gym (37 goes to almost an hour), and months you've been doing it (two months sounds so much longer than six weeks). This type of exaggeration is an art the Posh Mom uses to rev it up. And if she begins to take her own overstatements as truth, she may actually achieve those numbers the next time out. Visible results are also candidates for inflating—after a set of twenty push ups, next up is convincing yourself in your mind's eye that you see muscle demarcation in your bicep.

Posh Nutrition

For the PM who is always eating on the run, a good detox-ification is in order. Sugar highs and lows are okay for those with time to rest when they hit bottom. Unfortunately, you put kids down for naps but never get a chance to take a mid-day plunge into the down comforter yourself. Prevent the crash and burn setup by steering clear of those kitchen cabinet carbs that won't provide enough energy to take you through a crazy day: swear off red licorice, stop popping the pretzels, and pawn off the chocolate chip cookies to the playmates your kids bring home.

The health food store is where a Posh Mom starts the evolution from sugar queen to green goddess. A greens drink with spirulina and other goodies straight from the sea can replace your early-day coffee if you're trying not to fall victim to caffeine. With lots of protein and little sugar, health bars like Zone Perfect (we like chocolate peanut butter), Pria Complete Nutrition (our fave is French vanilla crisp), and Luna (you've got to try the caramel nut brownie) can make you glad you sunk your teeth into them—rather than into the scraps from the seemingly "Happy Meal" your kids are eating.

Scarfing the veggies holds the key to keeping regular (*such* a grandmother conversation), plus it impresses the little ones who hear you preaching the vegetable gospel, and who will get wise quick if they've never seen you consume a one. Cut up and cart them along in little plastic baggies—you may feel like your kids, but at least you're foregoing the brown paper bag with your name written on it, and come on, your body will thank you. That way, in the midst of all the frenzy your schedule creates, there won't be an eating frenzy with garbage food you grabbed fast.

Let's face it, though, no matter how much we go on about super green powers to our children, they do get boring quickly (shhhh, don't let your kids read this). Keep stamina snacks in the car for when you need a bit more pizzazz: almonds, popcorn, and raisins will help ward off the urge to binge on the leftover, half-eaten, almost-melted peanut butter cup your daughter handed you after it fell on the floor of the car.

A Pill a Day... ● ● •

To keep on top of her game (and her kids' game schedules), a PM needs to down her vitamins. Sometimes her day doesn't allow for a shower, so even five minutes to set the pills out and gulp them seems like four minutes too long, plus there's not a bit of instant gratification in the deed. If your motto is that teeth were made for chewing and nothing should be in your throat before it's gone through that process, the task becomes even more tedious. Investigate the spray vitamins that are sweet tasting and simply spritzed under your tongue. The results in your energy and youth aren't any quicker than their horse-pill cousins, but if it gets you to follow through, who cares?

Water ● ● ●

Posh Moms have a stubborn stickler side that can result in an all-or-nothing mode. Many of us forego drinking water because it's been hammered in that anything less than eight glasses just won't do. If we can't do that, we'll do nothing. Other excuses for a bone-dry day are: "I detest public bathrooms" and "Diet Coke counts." Sure, your body will keep you toilet hopping when you first start the regimen, but you'll soon regulate. And diet soda, while a liquid, can only be counted on for bloat. So start chugging the H_2O. As any PM knows, water isn't only for sipping—it's also her purest accomplice in her quest for smooth skin, a killer bod, and brain cells functioning at the highest percentage possible. Drag your filled-to-the-brim bottle to the gym, to the flag football field (share your spout with no one, except your kids of course), and to your late-day meeting. It'll keep you hydrated and perky—not to mention radiating across the conference table.

> ### Poshmom.com Pick
> Sprayology vitamins are a yummy way to mist away and tackle any and all of a mom's unique needs, like pre-menstrual moods, post-baby plump, and even hormonally broken-out faces. Oh, and they have a basic multi-formula as well.

Wine ● ● ●

At long last the kids are in bed and the cabernet is calling your name. Go ahead and answer it—if you can answer "yes" to all of the following:

- In the previous twenty-four hours there were no complaints of nausea and/or an urge but inability to vomit by any and all residents of the house under the age of eighteen.
- The things on your "to-do" list for the following day can be transferred to the next day (given the penchant for one glass to turn into one too many).
- The last time you bragged "my kids always sleep through the night" was over one month ago and the jinx is no longer in effect.

If you've answered in the affirmative to all three, break open the bottle and unwind. If not, keep it corked and resort to an herbal tea instead.

Unleaded Tea ● ● ●

Iced or hot, brewing this beverage, especially the decaffeinated members of the genre, has oodles of benefits. A PM can have a luxe pick-me-up with it anytime because it's packed with wellness. (She can even drink up when preggers.) And there's one to meet every time of day: earl grey for first thing; mint medley for a nooner; sweet dreams (a cozy blend of chamomile and hibiscus) before bed. Take your steeped potion with lemon for an added kick or the proper British way with cream and sugar (low-fat milk and Splenda will do if that's how your diet veers, although this would be for your taste buds' pleasure only, since scientists are questioning the benefits of tea when dairy is thrown into the mix).

Poshmom.com Pick

Mighty Leaf Tea bags make the paper-stapled, crumpled-leaf supermarket variety look unworthy of your rare and eked-out sipping time. Each pouch is made of stitched mesh fabric and houses whole leaf blends of enticing tea flavors like Green Tea Tropical, White Orchard, and Rainforest Mate. So pretty, they could double as potpourri.

Need a Jolt? ● ● •

When posh is petering and at dangerously low levels, you crave something and you want it administered intravenously. Three ideas:

1. Caffeine has a bad rap, but it is one we are willing to ignore when it comes down to the fact that we'll be down for the count if we don't use it. Caffeine can mean a mean cup of mud but it doesn't have to. Steeping up a mug of Green Tea instead of pouring a cup of espresso will feel healthier, thanks to the antioxidants lumped with the jolt. You may be just dressing it up differently to fool yourself, but you're entitled.

2. A Posh Mom is also a connoisseur of the fine points of chocolate. She gets that chocolate wafers are off the list (too much processed white flour) but the pure stuff is on, and right at the top. Not enough can be said about chocolate's royal ability to turn a bad day blissful, and the best part is that now any magazine you pick up tells you it's good for you. Well, maybe not for your thighs, but certainly for your mood and heart. So stash some in the one inside pocket of your bag the kids still haven't discovered and siphon off the chocolate from their Halloween or Valentine's loot.

3. Certain Posh Moms (we all dread eating with them) possess something more coveted than any bag or shoe on the market. It's the "able to eat devil dogs and not gain weight" speedy metabolism. Most of us lament having left that behind along with the ability to wear mini skirts cut "up to there." But no matter, any PM sees the importance of occasionally letting loose on a well-stocked vending machine. Your husband and kids are depending on your good mood, and sometimes it takes chewy caramel to do the job that trail mix just wouldn't get done.

Feeding the Troops ● ● •

Did you hear correctly? Did hubby just ask what you did all day, and why you're not cooking dinner? Well, let's see:

You delivered kid to school, escorted other kid to music, served lunch, discovered leak, plugged up leak, dealt with minimum six hissy fits, planned fit-thrower's birthday party, and installed and learned to play a G-rated computer game. A home-cooked meal just wasn't on the agenda and, by the way, neither was peeing.

You make a quick decision between divorcing him on the grounds of complete ignorance for all you do, or, like the true superstar you are, you search out the new and closest dinner-assembly store, like Dream Dinners, Super Suppers, and Let's Dish. If none of these are yet in your neck of the woods (or belly of your city), keep checking, they're bound to be there soon. The ingredients are already shopped for and chopped, you cook them up in their kitchen—leaving all the prep and cleanup to someone else for a change—and in a mere two hours, walk out with a couple of weeks' worth of meals for your freezer. Ask the friend you've been playing phone tag with to tag along and balance your want to socialize with your family's need to eat. Now cries from the troops for a home-cooked dinner can be answered even though your day out of the house ended minutes before the plates should be hitting the tabletop.

A Step Closer to Home Cookin' ● ● ●

If your good old mum was famous for her super agile finger that phoned daily for a pickup or delivery order but your American dream is yelling "dinner's ready with scents wafting through the house," then you're a Posh Mom who doesn't consider cooking your toil but your ta-da. This Posh Mom is elated by her family gathered round and the "yums" and "mmms" that ring out during mealtime. Still, the day holds a million missions, and she knows there has got to be a shortcut to the glory. Order your ingredients online the night before, and have that service or supermarket deliver them the next day, timed to arrive just when you hit the end of your workout.

Arts and Leisure

Squeezing a little culture into the life of a busy mom isn't easy unless it has something to do with the lacto-type found in the Go-gurts. She's relieved that she never again has to raise her hand in a class or write a report on something she lacks interest in, but that doesn't mean she has lost all interests.

Without being ashamed that her arts smarts have dissipated, she takes in what she may. Reading a small excerpt about a sculpture exhibit she would never have missed in a former life sometimes will have to suffice when the museum she loves is located out of town or even too far across town. Nutcracker performances with the kids may replace buying tickets for The American Ballet if show times for the Nutcracker correspond better with nap times—a PM knows what's in her best interests. Hardcover novels by praised authors will serve as eye candy on her bookshelves while an easy read chick-lit is lighter for her bag as well as for her psyche.

And Now, the News ● ● •

If there's no more water-cooler convo in your life—or even if there is, you'll need celeb mags to be able to chime in when the roundtable is in session on which of the latest starlet's boobs are fake or which Hollywood couple is teetering on the verge of divorce. All moms need a bit of star gossip to feel as if someone's life is nuttier than her own. For best results, though, don't boldly buy a glossy off the shelves—wait until you're a captive audience at the nail salon for the ultimate mix of mani and mindless.

And don't think that's all the "news" you'll need. It's not only posh to be informed, your young ones will repeatedly question you about the past and the present, and will count on you to provide answers. "Let's Google it when we get home" will only work so many times. The Posh Mom never condones her offspring cheating, but that doesn't mean her seniority (and/or senility) hasn't earned her the right to cut corners in her own clandestine way. A magazine like *Time* or *Newsweek* will sum up the week in a jiffy, and now that the noble Posh Mom Katie Couric delivers the world's news, it's a must to watch at least three times a week. What's more, nuke knowledge can actually ground the neurotic up-in-arms mom—the fact Iran has a nuclear program makes it explosively apparent to the PM that little Jimmy's fight with his kindergarten peer is not an issue after all.

Movie Rules

Kid appropriate (rated PG and G)
Try to gear them toward one you've heard has witty dialogue that might at times go over the kids' heads but will also make the grown-ups chuckle.

Chick-flicks—any film that has these girls as stars qualifies: Jennifer Aniston, Jennifer Lopez, and Kate Hudson
1. See on weekdays only with girlfriends.
2. Never drag your husband, or leave yourself subjected to losing movie-choosing privileges.

Action—anything that makes you recall Rambo, just with more technologically advanced effects
Purely for appeasing your husband. Try to plan one after a particularly hectic week when you wouldn't mind a snooze in the darkened theater (just remember ear plugs).

Tearjerkers—films with dying mothers, spouses, or worse, dying children
Steer way clear of these. Best left for NMs who don't leave anyone little behind if they go.

Hit the Books ● ● •

How many self-help books for moms are written by childless women with lots of psychological training but no experience caring for kids? Nevertheless, some have that authoritative tone from which we might actually glean some good points. But don't feel guilty if you don't heed the advice—perhaps the only worthwhile psychobabble is to focus on yourself by reading whatever the heck you want. For a Posh Mom, that could mean juicy novels, magazines to appease her vanity, or the autobiography of a posh bombshell she aspires to be.

Literary Agents ● ● •

Book clubs are a wonderful way to get together with friends for a higher purpose. Plus you get to do all the things we love to do, like discuss feelings, give opinions, freely gossip about unsavory characters, and talk, talk, talk. If you're finding yourself tiring of those grandstanding women who read every word, have way too much time to analyze, and

Posh Picks: Reads We Love

Juicy novel
Accidental Happiness

Biography
America's Queen: The Life of Jacqueline Kennedy Onassis (the poshest mom ever)

Magazines
Allure
Self
In Style
Real Simple
Lucky/Shop, etc.
W (great for leafing through for translating ideas)
New York Times/USA Today (for keeping current on news besides fashion)

convince everyone in the room that their take on the metaphors are the only ones, then politely excuse yourself from that group and start your own—think about one with your daughter, your daughter's friends, and your friends with their daughters. If your daughter is a new reader, you can do the reading together—and isn't that good quality time?

Back to School ● ● •

Did pregnancy catch you midway into your masters, when you soon decided that a B.A. was good enough? Or is pottery your passion (but it wasn't listed in your college catalog)? Then check out local continuing education classes in your town. Signing up will stimulate dormant brain lobes and make you feel like a giddy schoolgirl again.

Rated R Conversation ● ● ●

You spent the entire day speaking in G (with the occasional PG moment), and now you finally arrive at cocktails, dressed sans drool and among a sea of other adults. Yes, you're proud of your day with the kids, handling tantrums with major cajoling and stroking of mini egos, shopping for school clothes (conflicting fun since there wasn't even one little garment for you in any of the bags), and remembering what carpool you were supposed drive where, now be posh enough to compartmentalize and speak to the party crowd about something other than playdates and potties. Ever the PM, give your opinions on the current administration and voice your thoughts on war and other atrocities so eloquently that no one even suspects that just an hour ago you were wielding a dirty diaper and in full baby-babble mode.

Good Posh Manners

Part of a Posh Mom treating herself right is treating others right—and feeling damn good about it. Whereas before she prided herself on speaking her mind, now she needs to remember that what she says is representative of her entire family's reputation. The PM is wary of committing societal faux pas, and although she's an independent *chiquita*, she doesn't shun a little chivalry when offered.

Setting a Posh Example ● ● •

Manners and decorum are stepping stones to social prowess, and the Posh Mom smiles at those who can't seem to muster a grin and is gracious with both landscapers and ladies at lunch (without ever making a distinction). She goes to great lengths not to hurt others' feelings, even if that means sacrificing what she's really wanting at the moment—that's just who she is. She would never snub a fellow mom kneeling next to her at the sandbox just because she or her counterpart was not looking up to snuff. As grateful as she is for the ten-minute down and dirty catch-up session she's about to share with her best friend at a local cafe, if she catches a lonesome casual friend unwrapping an egg white wrap, she would invite her to join in on their banter.

She's always had a basic grasp of manners, but as a mom she has brushed up on the etiquette of everyday living because it's a precursor to walking with her head held high among her peers and to expecting such manners of her children. "If you have nothing nice to say, don't say anything at all," a Posh Mom whispers into tiny ears. Admittedly it's tough to practice this bit of preaching yourself, but as a PM, you have no choice but to be conscious of the damage that witchiness toward others can wreak.

A Posh Mom makes certain to refrain from the three "S's"—swearing, smearing, and slinging, as in mud. PMs know that they must set an example for that small permanent audience that has more keen hearing than the impression their small ears give, and so PMs abstain from nastiness (very unbecoming), and once-avid subscribers to good scandals are now defectors. She won't speak negatively about others (even if the dirt is frankly fitting) because she needs to have a clear conscience to be setting her kids straight when their own "s" words—like "stupid" and "sucky" debut at her dinner table. She has simply mastered participating in benign gossip only. Anything else is a misuse of her time and frankly it's not posh—it's twelve years old.

The PM's intact ego lets her easily tune out criticism and eliminates a need to talk back. After all, who has the hours or the desire to bring others down when they are busy being happy? The Posh Mom has made great choices: She's one half of a spectacular pair, dotes on her kids but doesn't relinquish all pre-kid interests, and still manages time on the phone for her best friend in need even if her own plate is so heavy at the moment it may just shatter. Most of all, she is a woman humbled by and grateful for this gift called motherhood.

Posh Predicaments

1. Predicament:
You've scheduled a playdate with your son's new friend. The day of the playdate, one of your good friends needs a favor for the afternoon—for you to take her child, too (your child's good bud but not good in a threesome).

Posh response:
Assure her of her ranking on your would-always-help-out list, but explain, without any hemming and hawing that would leave her wedge-in room, why today can't be a pinch-hit day. Blame it on the fact that your child has been better with one-on-ones lately (even when it's actually hers who can't handle the playdate *a trois*).

2. Predicament:
The PTA just phoned, requesting your volunteer services to chair yet another committee. Having just come off the chair of the last major school fund-raiser and differing greatly with the opinions of a few on the committee, you don't want to say no, but you have to.

Posh response:
A Posh Mom is no derelict, and she never feigns sickness for herself or her children in order to skirt responsibility—she takes it head on. Trust your instinct that you need a break and be honest about it. Tell them you'll pass on this one (no reason required), but to feel free to give a buzz when they're gearing up for the next. Go girl, you've avoided a crash and burn (yours) and a clash of the titans.

3. Predicament:
A nice guy thinks your husband is the coolest, but unbeknownst to him, the compliment is not completely returned (you can't particularly blame your guy). The "friend" is planning an elaborate guys' birthday bash for your hubby and wants to enlist your help.

Posh response:
Knowing full well hubby is always up for a party but would not particularly be pleased with one thrown by Mr. Wrong, you gush with appreciation at his thought but gently turn it down with a white lie that your man does not like the focus on him and that a party would make for a very unhappy birthday. Suggest instead a dinner—relegate it to Wednesday—for the four of you to go for a quiet celebration.

4. Predicament:
Your department head is going out on maternity leave—and the send-off party is the same eve as your daughter's ballet recital. You want to be supportive but can't miss the show.

Posh response:
Head out the door not a minute later than you have to in order get home and help your little one get dressed, but not before contacting Western Union to order a telegram delivered to the restaurant that reads: ALL THE BEST (STOP) WISH I WAS THERE (STOP) CAN'T WAIT TO HAVE YOU JOIN ME IN POSH MOMHOOD (STOP). This blast from the past is way more personal than any blurb on the community wish-you-well card ever is.

5. Predicament:

A potential new posh pal invites you to sit with her posse at a charity luncheon. You call to let her know you've sent in your donation, and she bids you a "great—have fun" farewell with no mention of the aforementioned seat beside her.

Posh response:

You've already sent in your money for a good cause, so go with it. Either sit with others you know or chat up others you meet there—you can give a wave and crack a smile from across the room to the take-back invite giver. Grudges don't suit you. She's obviously not the prospective friend you had pegged her for, and you don't have time for such pals.

6. Predicament:
On the day of your son's pre-school graduation, your daughter was nonstop complaining about her "stomachache" after her morning of running around feeling A-OK. You boldly told her to stop faking. She answered with a very public blowing-chunks episode amid the celebration. Okay, you were way wrong on this one.

Posh response:
Crying and groveling for forgiveness is not above a Posh Mom in this instance. It's required. She needs to admit wrongdoing—especially to her beloved offspring.

The Best Pick-Me-Up Ever

The daily minor catastrophes a mom endures are wearisome, even for this renaissance lady. You forgot to send your son's lunch, remembered at 2:00 p.m. your 2:15 p.m. teacher conference, and barely eked out the second half of yoga class, managing just a few cobra stretches. Twenty-four hours just doesn't cut it for your way full day. But all your disappointments can be erased with an "up-y" hug and one kiss from a set of tiny lips. The only tasks that truly need tending and attendance are little snuggle sessions between the PM and her petites.

Chapter Three

Relationships

Taylor's morning showers were anything but a simple time for a shampoo and a shower-gel leg shave. She used the mist to get herself clean on the outside and to get her head cleared and cleansed on the inside. Whether it was organizing call lists for the day or imagining the start-up of that party favor business she knew would be a success, she used the seamless glass as her very own think tank.

This morning was sure to be an especially skin-pruning one, as she was going to send her first child on the bus to kindergarten, and that would take some long and hard soul-searching.

There wasn't much she recalled about her own childhood, but this was a day she remembered easily, as she did not handle transitions well when she was young.

Nevertheless, she was getting her mind set to send off her child like a pro. She knew if any tears would be shed it would be done now, and they would drain away before her "baby" could spot them. She would emerge from the shower as someone who could instill strength in her child, not as a weepy mommy. Taylor wanted to say all the right "last words" so her first bird to fly off didn't have the same fears and experiences as she did. If she could plot it all out correctly, the day would be filled with discovering new bus buddies, finding friends to romp with at recess, and exploring the school building with giddy anticipation—and not with the stomachaches and fear she had years ago. So Taylor searched for the right words and memorized a speech to be given over scrambled eggs. She just hoped she could hold back the tears while she recited it.

The dialogue rocked, with lines like "you have an amazing personality, you can make new friends with whoever you sit with on the bus," and "there's nothing to be nervous about because everyone is in the same boat and new to the school." But no one at the breakfast table could make out what she was saying through the crying.

Then something happened that Taylor wasn't banking on. Her son jumped out of his seat, grabbed his backpack, and gave a peace sign as he ran out the door to climb on the bus. Okay, so her performance wasn't quite as stellar as she hoped, but obviously her timid genes were not part of the makeup of this child. She had two years to prepare for the next one—and a lot less pressure knowing that as time goes by her impact is not the one that always matters most.

Integrating Others

Rewind a few years to when you loved only yourself. "First comes me, then myself, and finally I" could be heard throughout your hallways. It was never labeled selfish (at least not by you), because it just felt heavenly, and you didn't know any better. Now with children on the scene and those days a distant memory, your main focus has done a one-eighty. No longer do the top entries on your list revolve around you. In fact, more days than not, your name is altogether absent. That's because family is the Posh Mom's priority, and you make plenty of time for yours. Add to the mix your other titles: wife, daughter, daughter-in-law, and best girl friend, and you've got lots of hats to wear, sometimes piled so high at once that they teeter, in danger of toppling. Some of them are stranger to pair up than others: talking personal with your group of tightest friends and turning nonchalantly to cover your son's mouth as he spews spitballs across the table, or turning up your skills in the kitchen to please your mother-in-law and later that day wanting to please that same mother-in-law's son in the bedroom. But armed with priorities in the right order, a Posh Mom swaggers on.

The Fruits of Your Labor

A PM is downright devoted to her kids. Her planner may be packed with committee meetings, business lunches, dealings with a decorator (or conversations spent convincing her other half of the need for one), training sessions, and more, but she would abruptly cancel or reschedule without blinking a mascara-clad lash if a call came from the school nurse about her little one's bellyache. The Posh Mom makes it a priority to show and tell her children that they top her list—anytime, anywhere.

During her lifetime, the most unique and ever-changing relationship the PM will have is the one she has with her kids. While you are aspiring to live The Posh Mom Life, your kids already think you lead it. To them you need no work: you are their queen, you are the prettiest, the smartest, the funniest. You're the one they look to when they make a joke to see if you're laughing (better crack that smile before the glance turns to a fit).

And for you: from their birth you will be faced with a lifetime of choices. What will you

> If you bungle raising your children, I don't think whatever else you do well matters very much.
> —Jacqueline Kennedy Onassis

and won't you do for them? It started even before they arrived. When pregnant did you drive right past Starbucks because you wanted a caffeine-free neonate? Or maybe you deemed your morning cup of joe was too vital to give up for the calm nerves of a baby. Your days as matriarch will keep your brain busy teetering on many more decisions, both big and small, and weighing out the most desirable alternatives.

No Right or Wrong ● ● •

There's a plethora of information out there on parenting, including the twenty-four hour search engine with millions of packed pages so easily accessed. We're expected to keep an arsenal of know-how about discipline, health, and education in the file cabinet called our brain—whose function has been severely debilitated by the hormones of pregnancy (and post pregnancy). Everyone, including our friends, is mistakenly counting on us to whip out this data when necessary, for our children and theirs. But this new phenomena of facts has the disadvantage of making us very accountable, which can be daunting. Mistake is a very big word, especially in the parenting department. The Posh Mom's solution—don't use it. Call them snafus, less letters and it sounds less intimidating. And just how you preach to your kids that "everyone makes them," don't be hard on yourself if what you thought was right at the time turns out to be wrong.

Our mothers had excuses for not knowing—practically zero information available with only one expert (Dr. Spock, whose ears resembled nothing of the *Star Trek* character). Still, what our mothers did wrong are those slip-ups we vow never ever to repeat. We won't stop a Play-Doh landscape in the kitchen because Daddy is coming home. No, daddy will need to take a giant step over it to get to the table for dinner. We also won't yell to get across what we want (max we'll go to is a very raised voice). Recalling how we shrunk from shrills, we won't partake even if that means we have to count to three, ten, or one hundred. We'll go as high as we must until we resurrect our sweet Posh Mom self and stifle the insane pathological one.

1 + 1 = too little time (for neuroses)

As the Posh Mom's family multiplies, so does her posh prowess. After child number one, the poor thing was still trying to strike a perfect balance. With age and more offspring, the scales tip more in her favor. Every walk, meal out, and admissions process doesn't have to be so high strung—it can just be a high. Now isn't it high time for that?

Scenario

The only pacifier you brought out today for your newborn drops sucky side down at the park.

First Child

Wince and then reluctantly institute the five-second rule, only after you've tried your own sterilization method with an anti-bacterial wipe from the diaper bag.

Ever After

Wonder "Is that his?" as you stare at a familiar-looking plastic knob on the ground. When recognition sets in, you happily pick it up (and think it's better for them to be exposed to germs early on), rub it on your pant leg as you forgot to pack the wipes, and offer it back up. Five seconds, five minutes, five hours—no difference, it's not a grody bathroom floor, it's nature, and you love the outdoors.

Scenario

It's time to change the diaper again, for a change.

First Child

The portable nylon changing pad is always on the don't-leave-the-house-without-it checklist, on hand to protect the car interior and other people's furniture when visiting, and, most important, to save their little tushy from the germ-infested drop-down changing table in public restrooms. The diaper's Velcro tabs were perfectly aligned and there was never ever a speckola of nastiness left on the pad or in pudgy leg folds.

Ever After

The pad has long been passed off—and written off—as a yucky germ-breeding mat that is not at all necessary to schlep around. Now you go for something that's more disposable, something that's right there and handy—a paper towel will do just fine, thanks. And since you're experienced enough to do it one-handed now, you can multi-task, returning a phone call or two in the process.

Scenario

With no after-school activities on the calendar this afternoon, you've been approached by a mom whose child wants a playdate with yours.

First Child

A spying session and interview are required to find out if the potential playmate has up-to-snuff qualities from which your child can benefit.

Ever After

If the offer is made, and your child vouches for his friend (and you go with it despite his 30—give or take—years less experience in the perception department), you agree and promise to call and check-in (from your cell phone under the steam of the facial you'll now be able to sneak in).

Scenario

Your kid's friend offers up a stick of gum to your virgin gum chewer.

First Child

Horrified, you stop your child's hand mid-reach and quiz the corrupter about whether his parents are aware of this vice.

Ever After

What a good sharer and nice friend he's made, you think, making sure you remind your son to chew it with his mouth closed.

Scenario

Before your little one even talks, people in town are

starting to talk about how to get in to that "prestigious" preschool.

First Child
You put on your teacher's hat, turn reading time from fun to fundamental by replacing picture books with flash cards, and make mealtime about math with a multiplication table place mat.

Ever After
You realize that preschool is not a precursor to a higher education, and you look for one that serves good snacks and will further your kid's social life—and it doesn't hurt that your mommy friends send their kids there, too.

Give 'em the Good Stuff— but What Does *That* Mean? ● ● ●

The moment the doctor hands you that precious baby, you must decide whether to put his or her suction to your nipple or cover up quick and search for a bottle. If you decide to dive into the formula tin, are you risking autism or a non-thriving child? Back in the day, breast was not best, but now it's so favored people may think you evil and selfish if you voluntarily deny your child. The poshest moms know not to get themselves caught up in public opinion. Even her day-old baby would sense her unhappiness if she was turned into an unwilling feeding machine. What makes your baby happy and healthy are the same things that have you feeling good, not just the colostrum in your breast milk.

When your kids start on supermarket foods, the organic or pesticide-laden question will catch your attention at mommy-and-me groups, on online forums, and in the latest issue of your favorite magazine you only have time to buzz through. Obviously no sane mother wants her family ingesting harmful chemicals, but at the same time, you did grow up (and pretty decently) eating them. Also spinning off this discussion is whether you will be a veggie pusher or a sweets and junk-food enabler. No doubt sugar is garbage, but it's also the best bribe in town if you don't abuse it. When in the fitting room, one leg into that last pair of pants and with a complaining child, finding a lollipop in your bag can buy you ten more minutes. That simply won't work with a bag of snow peas.

Cook's Kitchen ● ● •

An NM's schedule can be packed straight through dinner and beyond—maybe some drinks, possibly a party. As a Posh Mom, though, she needs to slow down midafternoon to make time to make something in her kitchen—at least a few days a week. If the pizza man recognizes your voice on

Posh Picks: At-Home Activities

You haven't forgotten about:
- the backyard: Frisbees, footballs, and hula hoops
- board games and floor games like Twister and Boggle
- bopping around the kitchen to music (see page 51 for tunes you and your little guys can agree on)
- the remote. You certainly are not placing them in front of a TV and bidding farewell, but a little glassy-eyed downtime with some Discovery Kids programming or even fun-loving cartoon characters won't damage them, either.

the phone and completes your address for you, it's a sign you've been ordering in too much. When you're done wielding the spatula, whether you're lucky enough to make one meal to serve on everybody's plate or you're working multi-burners with something different in every sauté pan for the picky eaters in the crowd, sit down with the kids while they dine. You'll get some good insight into their day and some insurance for their future: studies show sitting down as a family for dinner at least once a week means kids are less likely to go down an ugly path.

Afternoon Hustle and Bustle ● ● •

Somewhere between overscheduling and opting out is usually a Posh Mom's best plan of action for after-school activities. It's truly best not to go to extremes on this one. The overzealous sign-them-up-for-everything mom believes that exposure to it all will result, no matter how pooped everyone is at the end of the day, in tomorrow's Tiger Woods. That belief is so passé; the PM much prefers striving to keep her kids learning and happy but not to the point of a juvenile mental and physical breakdown (or juvenile detention for that matter). Look for your kids to experience something, don't just look for something to do.

I Want to Be a... ● ● •

Every child has a dream, which may come to them unbidden during the night or gently forced down their little throats during the day. Maybe he wants to be a commercial fisherman (after his weekend fishing trip with dad) or she wants to be a makeup counter salesgirl (after a trip to the department store with you). Whatever the case, a PM never squashes her kids' fantasies, no matter how unlucrative you may judge them to be. Spurred on by all those parents we know who switched careers midlife, we're telling our kids to shoot for the stars they want. Good for us. When we were young, our mothers told us many things we have to

> Mama exhorted her children at every opportunity to "jump at de sun." We might not land on the sun, but at least we would get off the ground.
> —Zora Neale Hurston

thank her for. Yet also thanks to her wise words about career choices, we are not the famous singer, circus star (okay, this one we'll give her), or President we hoped to be. "Being a dancer is too risky. A sprained leg and it's all over," or "Who makes money singing in a band?" could be heard in our homes, and out of respect we suppressed the obvious retort: "Journey, Foreigner, Chicago, duh?"

We know the odds are just as low now, but the Posh Mom is in tune with helping her children set their sights on what makes them happy. Sure, she needs to fight the urge to bite her nails as she tolerates them finding their own little ways. But she refrains from setting each and every stone in their path, stretching the umbilical cord to lengths she would never have expected by telling them "go for it" when her own fears (especially the unfounded ones) leave her aching to say "hold back."

Together Time ● ● •

A Posh Mom understands that pure and clean outdoor fun—swinging a bat or sitting on a swing—are the kind of simple times they'll cherish. In order to relate to most kids, you've got to get chummy with grass and make nice with the sprinkler even if they're not your favorite play-mates. Don't be opposed to sweating it out with them even if it means an extra shower for you before bed. A game of red rover, ring around the rosie, or dodge ball can substitute for a workout that you didn't manage to get in this morning. No matter the age, it's the bike rides and the catching fireflies they will always remember.

If air conditioning and carpet is more your speed, try to get over it—at least for a span of minutes. Give them the fresh air they deserve, then coax them inside. Try a fresh batch of arts and crafts supplies to make Valentine's day decorations for the house, a 360-piece puzzle that will take a long, silly afternoon to complete, or the makings for cookies (including rainbow sprinkles) they can bake with you. No emails or PDAs, though—the only electronics a PM is concerned with when she's frolicking with little Poshies are the timer and the oven light her kids are flicking on and off as they are perpetually "just checking."

Until the chocolate chips are melted, she knows the merit of the overdue library book. Thank goodness libraries are lenient and charge low fees to scatter-brained moms who are well schooled in the importance of reading to their cubs but who don't fret the due dates. (Although she does make it a point to be a stickler for books on loan from school, lest her little ones get branded as late with loaners—no way is she subjecting them to that shame.)

Biology is the least of what makes someone a mother.
—Oprah Winfrey

And back home, she stocks her kids' shelves with favorites: fairy tales like *Sleeping Beauty* for her fairy princess, Dr. Seuss books like *Green Eggs and Ham* for her little riddler, first books for her baby (*Goodnight Moon*), and for the whole crowd, charmers straight from her childhood she just has to pass down so she knows that her kids' fingers are patting the same soft white bunny hers did so many years earlier.

Get Out the Luggage ● ● •

A family vacation is another biggie in the memory department. But good memories are made from fun—not forced behavior. Stop envisioning travel to multitudes of museums, far-off lands of culture like Europe and Asia, and archaic treasures and ancient sites. A Posh Mom has different strategies to keep her hip kids happy on the vacay. One is to visit a childless aunt in a city that's fun to tour. There's lots to see, and your kids will be showered with adoration— wild behavior is cute when it only comes to town once a year. Plus, you'll get to go out at night while auntie gets to play mommy. Another choice is anyplace with roller coasters and other amusement park institutions like the freefall, boardwalk carnival games (and the oversized stuffed animal prizes you don't want to lug home), and warm, powdery funnel cake. Anyplace such as Disneyland, Disney World, and Hershey Park will do (the added bonus with the latter is chocolate around every bend). A final fail-safe option is water (chlorinated or salted) and a noodle or boogie board. You'll think your children have sprouted gills by the amount of time they spend happily submerged.

To keep herself and hubby happy, all a PM needs is a kids' club. By no means is this a pawn-off to a baby-sitting service. Instead, its sole purpose is to be so fun for your kids that they beg to come back next year—and that you bask in your grownup time. After they're finished making candy-filled piñatas and learning about Mexican heritage and you've soaked up a good book and some sun, you all come back refreshed and ready to romp together.

Poshmom.com Pick

So what do you bring in the car or on the plane to keep creative fingers busy and out of the old armrest ashtrays? Take along Wikki Stix. Each pack is light and flat so it shoves easily into your carry-on and contains eight yarn-wax hybrid sticks that are colorful, twistable, and stickable. Yet they leave no mess on hands, clothes, or any wall or tray table, which delights moms and flight attendants alike.

If the hotel you choose doesn't offer this kids' oasis, put your own posh pursuits aside. Make the most of together time without incoming phone calls, emails, or salon visits. This means packing beauty accoutrements for maximizing time together. Don't forget gel for slicking back hair at the pool after a swim—the threat of bad hair should not stop you from diving in with the kids. Even if your least favorite princess is Ariel, you need to

take a requisite dip otherwise they won't remember anything from the entire vacation except the fact that you
would not dunk your head—and they'll tell everyone
back home about the non-escapade. Not worth it. A
leave-in conditioner for museum trips and a frizz tamer
for dining out will help you disconnect from your blow-
dryer for a few days.

You probably will not relax, nor read, nor shop on this
family trip, but the kids will have you all to themselves,
unfussed-over hair and all, and the video to prove it.

Your Guy

We all made promises, took oaths, and swore up and
down that we wouldn't let children change our marriage,
not even an iota. Witnessing the differences the third
part of "threesome" made in other pairs' lives made you
adamant that would never happen on your home front.
You'd stay united forever, make alone time no matter
what the week brought on, and remain in love and pas-
sionate lovers. You learned your lesson from friends who
were once-loving couples turned asexual because kids
claimed squatters' rights in their bed. Their example—or
lack of it—empowered you at 3 a.m. to walk your own
kids back to their bedrooms, even if you had to do the
walk in twenty minute increments all night until your
alarm clock finally put you out of your misery.

Then comes the day you're snapped awake by the reality that the "just the two of us" love got bundled in a package deal called "one big happy family." You knew full well you had to keep the friendship, love, and sexual verve cooking with your hubby. So what happened? The sex now fits into some weird predictable pattern, your friendship means you pass each other in the house (so technically you're now "friendly" not "friends"), and stolen smooches between the two of you never happen without "mommy look at what I did" in the background. When you look at him and think only of good times past, that's a major *problemo*—a relationship can't survive on memories when neither of you can even remember what day of the month it is. It's simply not okay.

And the Posh Mom never lets it get too far gone—she's keen on creating new memories keeping him hooked on her and her on him. Too many phone calls will slip through the busy cracks this week, but not the one to the baby-sitter so she and he can share some wine together (the kind you sip, not tune out). Quality couple time is not discretionary in a Posh Mom's world—she is a date night fanatic, and it would take close to a natural disaster to cancel her reservations. And those other nights of the week are anything but boring—whether it's pillow talk (after the kids are finally in bed) or a heated discussion (or heated sex, take your pick), a PM knows that moments just for he and she make for a content we.

Couple time is key. You both owe it to each other; after all you're equally responsible (well, okay, not equally, you were the one bloated and uncomfortable, although he did have to listen to you complain) for granting the gift of posh parenthood. And although it takes work to maintain your coupleness, luckily it's the type that's the pure fun variety.

Die-Hard Date Night ● ● ●

It's a must: a standing weekly time for the PM and her guy to leave the house without strapping anyone in the backseat—some forward-thinking Posh Mom from the past created it, but unfortunately, she was never credited in the history books. Establishing and sticking to date night is mandatory for getting back your coupleness—only a household virus or bacteria counts as a valid reason for cancellation. You can conjure up countless reasons not to go, most edged in some bit of truth. You're stressed because your five-year-old's cough is going on three weeks and the pediatrician has no answers. Your bed is looking irresistible because for the past three weeks the cough has been ringing in the hall and has you in bed but not sleeping. But a Posh Mom musters it up and goes—her marriage won't be number two to all things kids all the time.

You and hubby sneak off without other couples, without kids, and without even the baby who isn't speaking yet. Dinner, movie, walk on the beach. Any simple outing makes for serious improvement and investment in the relationship.

Looking at you, he sees a face pre-worry wrinkles and a body pre-pregnancy. You see a head fully stocked with hair and a stomach that hasn't turned into a gut. The passion level bounces back up to when you first met. If it sounds too idealistic, well, that's because it is. Any expectations that this date-night thing will be an instant fix should be left at home with the kids. Just indulge in the treat of uninterrupted adult conversation. It might be hard at first but soon it will come naturally, especially if you stick to a schedule—do it come hell or not-so-high fever. Think of date night as an insurance policy for hitting your silver, gold, platinum, and more anniversaries (and think of the gift potential!).

And the fun's not done when you get home. Hitting

Posh Picks: Date Night Agendas

1. Stuff that brings out the kid in you (but when the kids are around, you don't get to take your turn)
   - Miniature golf
   - Bowling
   - Amusement parks

2. Stuff that brings out the sexy mama in you
   - Couples massage
   - Wine tasting
   - Tango lessons

3. Things you remember your parents hiring a baby-sitter for:
   - The opera or ballet (or theater if he'll balk at no dialogue and men in tights)
   - Dinner at "your" restaurant
   - A drive-in movie and "parking"

the pillow straight away is not the Posh Mom's style. She'd much prefer pillow talk and then some. Sex is what technically made her a Posh Mom, after all, and its importance can't be ignored even if the day has been long and grueling. Order coffee with dinner and jump in the shower when back at home to start fresh. Even if you spot the bed and envision yourself cozy and bundled under the covers, you need to erase that easy-out picture, stop thinking, and just partake (hopefully you'll be "satisfied" you did). Making love is the one activity (besides maybe skiing) you can do together that will burn some calories and solder your relationship at the same time.

One Step Ahead of Him ● ● •

Initiate in bed. Yes, you read that right. No matter your level of sleep-deprived stupor nor the size of your under-eye bags, put the kids to bed, put on something very uncomfortable but very revealing, and start putting your mind in the gutter. When was the last time? If you paused to check your agenda, it's been way too long. This small move (or moves) will be a big-time deal to him, his ego, and his resuscitated attraction to you.

Surge the Urge ● ● •

A confident PM doesn't shy away from bringing something (never someone) new into the bedroom. Nothing as over the top as wigs or whips, but maybe just a little whipped cream or arousal oil (Zestra is topical and herbal). There are other things in the pharmacy aisles— like KY warming liquid and hot rod condoms complete with applicator so they take a mere second to put on— made just for helping you get in the moment and momentarily forget the permission slip that you still need to sign for your child's field trip the next day.

Soft Focus on Little Annoyances ● ● •

Only a bomb of a husband manages to be sweet, sappy, silly-willy with your kids while still "doing it" for you. And true to posh form, you snagged him as yours. You really are in the money (no matter your tax bracket) with a partner that perfect to go through life with. But as a Posh Mom, you appreciate his yays and are sharp enough to see his nays yet still roll with them—no value-added in zooming in on little idiosyncrasies. You may not be thrilled that he smokes an occasional cigar, but you dare not make it a topic with your best "couple" friends on Friday night. Never do you air dirty laundry

Poshmom.com Pick

A PM knows there's always two sides to every story, and she makes sure she's well read up on the opposing side. *Daddy Needs a Drink* by David Wilder offers insight on just how your man feels—although your guy may not admit to having feelings.

(shirts that smell like an ashtray included). And when girlfriend conversation turns to male-hating banter, you never participate—even if your hubby did piss you off just that morning. Talking badly about your soul mate is for traitors, not posh pairs.

Vacations for Two ● ● •

Date night is practice for the hopefully-more-than-once-a-year vacation without kids. Never happens, you say? Well, get on the horn with your travel agent and make it happen!

When planning your accommodations, go as luxurious as your wallet allows. Check out pictures of the bathrooms where you might be staying to make sure they are as nice or nicer than your own. This is a week of showering and lounging at last, not the usual clean and run. Another consideration is the hotel's children policy. Are they allowed? When yours are un-Velcroed from your side, do you really want to see, hear, or worse, be awakened early by anyone else's? They may play tag in the room above yours and foil your plan for re-creating the college days of sleeping until noon.

Let go

Hotel arranged, you book the next flight to Europe. But when flight time arrives, the thought of boarding a plane sans kids leaves you a little hesitant and feeling like you're reliving labor, with the stomach pains to prove it. Still, you've just got to go. Do you think they'll feel abandoned? Lucky for you, the experts on child rearing say you are actually teaching them a very important lesson in life. People, even their amazing, loving mother, leave—and then come back. Empower them by giving them a chance to be free-standing while giving yourself the power to sightsee until you have to hightail it to your spa appointment. This philosophy may sound too good to be true, but most all preschool teachers who coo "mommies always come back" agree. Owning that knowledge should help, even if the kids' antics get as bad as ankle-weighting and out-of-their-mind shrieking.

And you know deep down that sneezing and coughing are not a reason to call the airlines and cancel. Yes, kids are more needy when they are sick, but running noses, as sad as they are to look at (and gross if they're

Poshmom.com Pick

Luggage tags by Pamela Barsky help you spot yours in a jiffy and even get a little stress-relieving (the plane part of traveling is always grueling) giggle out of these funny, bright colored tags looped around the handles. They come six to a pack, are easy to identify, and each has a different saying, such as, "careful: my shoes are inside," "this is my bag," and for the return trip, "caution: dirty clothes inside." Plus there's room on the back to write all your info.

not yours), don't qualify as illness. Just look at any school in the winter months. It's filled with those "ill" children whose mothers needed to get some errands done. That said, a few boogies in the nose is not akin to vomiting and high fever. A trip to the doctor should make clear if your next call should be begging the hotel not to charge a cancellation fee or to request a vegetarian meal on the plane (so much better than a regular one). Always be sure to soothe your guilt by nailing down a special someone, be it grandmother, aunt, or favorite baby-sitter, to watch your little ones. They'll be able to wipe noses, give cough syrup, and administer the lovin' just as well you can.

If you were lucky enough to escape without disease, go with a clear conscience—and stay that way. The job of mothering knows no limits or boundaries. It's physical, mental, emotional, and 24/7 for the rest of your life. A vacation is the minimum you as a Posh Mom can do for yourself and for your husband. The worst you can do is get to your destination and pine for the tykes. His ego will be crushed, and who can blame him? A phone call a day is sufficient to scooch in a "we care" call while off and caring for your marriage. Doing so from a cell phone on a chaise at the beach, eyeing those beautiful waves, makes hanging up easier.

And don't forget that absence works miracles for behavior. You'll be a nicer person to them when you're reunited—and they'll do the same for you, especially when they see the stack of presents you dragged home. Believe us now? Enjoy. You, not the young ones, are the only one in danger of mental scarring if you don't relax and let go.

When you're off the clock

Resurrect the woman you were before stretch marks, even if it is for just a five-day stretch. Speaking of stretching, sleep in and then exercise. Without scheduling time for a breakfast negotiation, you'll have plenty of energy to get in a great workout. Eggs or oatmeal is someone else's culinary problem back home. Your morning plan is with your razor—today is your day to finally make no excuses for stubble. That's because your shower will be longer than a millisecond. Finally, steam will have a chance to form on the shower door while you deep condition your hair. And when it's soft and silky, blow-dry, iron, or curl it *and* put on a touch of makeup instead of making the pained choice between the two. Now that you're looking like a prize, you and your man could wander through a museum—remember, you don't have to worry if there's a pizza place nearby for the kids who are "starving." You might even want to just hang out and read a magazine front to back, to get back on an in-the-know track. It's like old times again. He's reading, you're reading. You're not reading the same material, but you're on the same page.

You can even break away for a bit: pamper yourself with a manicure and give him the pass to go off on his own without any guilt. No kids equal an unstifled schedule, even if you don't spend the entire time together. When your multitasking mind is allowed to roam, it shows up immediately on your skin—a free and more fun fix than slathering on the priciest cream you can buy. Take a look, the mirror reflects the change in your face already.

Back to the grind

Even before you re-enter your home state, the little ones are probably already creeping into your mind and whining in your dreams. Small but forceful, it's as if they sense your return is imminent—and they want back in. They may think you vulnerable to falling back into old habits when you sashay over the threshold, but Poshie post-vacation is fortified and now protected from a complete takeover.

Having reclaimed your bond, the two of you can attempt a conversation without interruption and be more poised to succeed. Let them just try asking Daddy for candy after you already said "no." Have a protest a *deux*, standing up for parents' rights to have control over the clicker. And a go at a midnight sprint into your bed will get a resounding "go back to your room" in unison. With any luck you may be doing something other than sleeping! Vacations always refresh the hormone flow—after a few days off, a mom feels like a sexual being and not an asexual errand runner.

The Grandparents

Your relationships with your parents and his enter a new dimension when they transform before your eyes into grandparents. They used to hang on your every word and accomplishment, but in the hospital it's immediately clear that's no longer so. No sweat off their backs if you got the epidural in yours or not, what they really want to know is when the doctor will be back to catch this baby when he or she pops out.

The changes spiral from there. Whether it's your set or his, no one outside your bloodline cares for your little ones with the fervor they do. You remember your dad as a strait-laced and stern taskmaster, but as grandpa he's smoochie, spoiling, and soft. When they visit, the conversation inevitably winds up about the grandchildren because the toddlers are the center of their world these days. Tell them how well you are handling being in charge of the charity luncheon and they'll politely listen, then give you an "okay, done with you...next!" look. They want the scoop on the poop—how many times a day and is it firm—and more important, is baby saying "grandmama" yet?

Nana, Nona, or Mom-mom ● ● •

Ignoring the fact that she actually answers to one of these pet names, you admit that your respect for the lady triples immediately after the nurse from the maternity ward is no longer at your beck and call. And with each kid your admiration grows exponentially. Stunned at all a tiny baby needs and how absolutely alone you are in answering all those needs, you imagine how it was for your mother. Your thoughts pop between "How did she do it?" to "I should have been nicer to her as a child." ("I can't believe she didn't tell me about the after pain of birth" is another quip you file for a future confrontation.)

She was always a little anxious when raising you, and you now know the source of that anxiety: *You.* But your mother survived a time when there were no guidebooks like "What to Expect in The First Year," nor even one Gymboree-type class. You've been put in your place and at the same time amazed that she emerged intact without the help of some doctor-prescribed meds. What's more, she managed to nurture you to be the Posh Mom you are today, despite all her era lacked. You make no claim to be first generation posh, just a posh descendant of her. Kudos to the Posh Grandma—always show her the respect she deserves: always return her phone calls within 24 hours, never allow the kids to play the favorite grandma game or pit grandparents against each other in present-giving status, and trust her judgment to be alone with the kids, even if you don't really have anywhere else to be.

That being said...

Remember how you couldn't do something because you were under her roof? Well now the roof belongs to you. When she's under it, however, she thinks she still rules the rafters. You're a woman with child (or children) now, which makes her advice harder to swallow and may just qualify as a choking hazard. Nevertheless she's there to dole it out: "hold the baby's neck more upright," "there aren't enough parameters for the kids," and, the inevitable "they eat an awful lot of sugar." Opinions about your parenting skills can be paralyzing and overwhelming.

If your mom was on the overprotective side, your goal might be anti-hover—you let your kids find their own way, to a point. You've hammered into them enough that biking and helmets go together and trust that they'll follow suit when at a friend's house for a playdate and off your watch. They're at said playdate without you because you've met the mother and determined she's got her wits about her. From the cluck of your mom's tongue, you surmise she disagrees. According to her, riding a bike is not necessary, and playdates need your presence, even if the other mother is a Rhodes Scholar. But a Posh Mom tries to bite her tongue.

When not possible, remember another old rule your mother taught ("it's not what you say but how you say it")? You have to skillfully let her know that these are now your decisions to make. Try something like "Mom, I know you thought it was best that I didn't eat a candy bar until my eighteenth birthday, but I'm giving them sweets in moderation so they don't wind up a raging chocoholic like me." If you have a mother who just can't take the hint and plays deaf when her opinion isn't the reigning one, it might pay to trick her into believing you're listening. When she's out of earshot, slip Sam the Skittles and share a sneaky smile. But hopefully she'll locate some sense or at least momentary respect for your decisions, and you won't have to resort to undercover operations.

Q&A: Amy's Worldly Goods

The situation:

The night before my parents departed for a trip to England, I rang them up to say "Cheerio!" I wished them safe travels and also slid in that it's not at all necessary to return home carting all sorts of stuff for me, hubby, and the kids as memorabilia from their continent hopping. I worry they'll be focused on finding just the perfect thing and won't enjoy their shopping forays. I fear they'll spend themselves silly and could have upgraded their hotel stay instead. I fret at the weight of the luggage (and the efforts necessary to zip it closed) caused by the loot. And I cringe at the thought (even though their taste is spectacular) of finding a home for the stuff they've dragged home. When they insist I not be a cad, what am I, a PM, to do to stop them?

The solution:

I understand that my yen to save them the hassle and save me from having to display some kitschy foreign bauble is eclipsed by their desire to spoil my family. I'm humbled that my offspring and I are always in their thoughts—even halfway across the world—and resign myself to the trinkets. But I do suggest they bear gifts for the kids only and drop hints about what they'll freak for, like a sparkly "London" scene to add to a growing snow globe collection or a miniature double decker bus to park with other official vehicles from around the world. These teeny items won't take up much space—in my folks' bags or once landed back at my home— and they're sold around every corner, so I'm not afflicted with guilt about my parents spending their time away from home hunting for it.

Supporting roles

No matter how much they may criticize, let's recognize and idolize our moms for what they are: the key to our freedom. We can rely on them for the usual support, guidance, and love and now, most important, for the baby-sitting. The guiltless liberty we get when leaving the kids with her doesn't compare to any other child care situation. Leaving your offspring with your mother is the closest thing to them actually being with you, even if reality is you're nothing alike. So, breathe a sigh of relief, and don't let the baby gate hit you on the way out.

The Other Mother ● ● •

If you are a member of the tiny percentage who feels true love for your mother-in-law, then you hit the jackpot and can skip the following tirade. Rarely is it such a happy story, and many times the tale goes like this: she liked every other girl in her son's life, but you snagged him and bore his children. Now she sees you as a quasi-enemy who stole not only her son, but who now controls the grandchildren. Your kids will sniff out the bad vibe she's emitting (they're always more in tune than they let on), and the rest of the family will sense the tension when you're all together: at your son's fifth birthday party, dance performances, elementary school graduations, and Thanksgiving. Obviously a less-than-posh attitude, but what can you do?

The Posh Mom who has earned respect from every-one in her life (spouse, children, friends, coworkers) does not grant any reprieves, even if the one trying to one-up her is the mother of her husband. So the answer is lots, including (just like you tell your kids) don't let her see she irks you, because the more she knows it, the more she'll do it. Try "right back at ya" but with a sugary sweet smile (all the while thinking, "I'm rubber and you're glue whatever you say bounces off me and sticks to you"). Tactic #2: Demand a united front from your husband. She'll know her place as soon as she's put there by her son/prince, demonstrating that he won't accept the insidious behavior. Once she's clear that he'll have none of it, the nonsense should stop—or at least subside somewhat.

Smotherhood ● ● ●

The opposite scenario can be equally upsetting, and handling it requires more finesse so as not to appear unkind or harsh. You know the drill: they love you so much that there are no boundaries in the relationship. They come, they stay, they don't know when to leave. Either your parents or his, they're pros at giving their advice and opinions, and you are left feeling that it may be worth cutting corners and spending less on your splurges to buy them an out-of-town vacation home. But then you know that they'll invite you to come stay there with them, so you reluctantly give up that idea. Thank goodness that it's good intentions they have, but they've just gotten a little forgetful. They've forgotten about their individual lives and the need for you and your husband

and your children to have yours. As idyllic as it may seem to spend all vacations as one big extended happy family, it's actually invasive and can't turn out well.

Subtly suggesting the need for privacy may work in lieu of the dramatic confrontation you're dying to unleash in moments of fury. Take an example—you're in the kitchen with MIL watching the kids romp out back when you gush about the Disney trip you and hubby have painstakingly planned. Wild animal lodge accommodations, intentions to fast pass Space Mountain three times in a row, and a breakfast with Alice in Wonderland and Mary Poppins. She wonders aloud how cheap airplane tickets would be for her and the FIL. Whoa, mama. Ain't gonna happen. Let your initial blood boil simmer, then gently break the news. "Mom, we really need to have breakfast alone with Alice and Mary as a nuclear family. But we promise to have breakfast with you right when we get back home so you can pour over the pictures and pick which ones you want."

Friendships

A Posh Mom's list of good friends is as pared down as the waistline of her daughter's Barbie doll. Not that there is any shortage of other moms clamoring for her attention—she is, after all, fun, funny, magnetic, and intensely loyal—but for her, friendship is all about quality, not quantity.

She's got no elbow room for warm bodies and pointless conversation (although she'll still be forced to do a bit of that if her husband's bonus is dependent on it).

The Posh Mom is at home with a network of acquaintances she rubs shoulders with on her very own runways (aka the sidewalks of town), and she can one-handedly socialize with an array of women, such as the moms of her children's classmates and the school bus stop ladies who chat her up. But she only discloses her deepest and darkest to a select few true blues. And the PM feels honored and lucky that these women (best guy friends went by the wayside when her hubby sent them there) are thick-and-thin there for her, and she, of course, returns in kind. Unwavering friendship bonds are Posh Mom safe havens, where gossip about each other is off-limits and confiding in one another means not needing to begin with "between you and me."

New at This ● ● •

If you were the first out of the gate to give birth, then you know how in a flash you were different from your friends without kids. The first hang-up mid-sentence due to panic caused by a screaming infant (hunger could kill a child, so we thought) solidified it. That your free-as-a-bird pal didn't get the urgency of the situation, if only in your own mind, made it clear. Welcome to your new world.

But things settle down, and a plan is set to get together and catch up with life's goings-on. Once a sharp lady, your profound ignorance about the world beyond the four walls of your house appalls her (and proves to be an eye-opener for you, too). You wish you could show off that you've at least got a handle on all things motherly so she'll want in on the club, but you can't pull the burp cloth over her eyes. Even if she can't actually see the raw nursing nipples that made you go braless, the Kegel performance in your seat just in case you sneeze, or the angst you feel about getting rid of your child's pacifier, she knows you too well. She can tell you're frazzled. Okay, so you know you didn't win this round; but as runner-up, you did gain the desire to get back in the ring. You know it's going to be hard fought but well worth your efforts, as day-by-day as they may be.

When you're buff enough to bridge your two universes of woman and mother, you acclimate and slowly step out to join civilization again. Sure, there are still differences, but the field is finally leveling a bit. Your childless friend may be more plugged into celebrity gossip, but does she know about the choice celebrity stroller and exactly how to collapse it? (She looks on befuddled and, she's got to admit, in awe.) She might have slinked in with the better outfit but you one-up her by miraculously controlling your flailing baby's fit in the restaurant. (Besides you know who makes her torso-hugging jacket, you just can't fork over the bucks until you lose the last of your baby weight.) Ever the posh new mom, you never let her lack of relating get confused with misanthropy. Her day will come when a little someone with lots of big needs will flip her life helter-skelter, and then there will be true understanding. Until then, you still dedicate your time to her, even if it is a hundred percent of your last five non-allotted-to-kids minutes of the day. You've started the next chapter, but that won't close the book on this friendship.

Members of the Club ● ● •

Girlfriends with kids are the PM's saviors, sounding boards for your elation and complaints about motherhood. They're your fellow soldiers who empathize and sympathize with your daily highs and breakdown lows. Maybe they're new confidants from a toddler music class or posh pals who date back to your high school days. Whatever the case, the fact that they have kids (regardless of if they're older or younger than yours) puts them in a place of competency to understand you. A non-mom (who changes her own clothes twenty times before she heads out the door) won't understand how you're driven to the edge when your five-year old struts down the stairs in her fifth outfit of the morning just as the school bus breezes by.

With these ladies, an unspoken pact is made. Every mother is allowed venting moments about her children, but it is not the stuff of which gossip is made. Until you become a mom, you don't know how strongly you can love someone other than yourself and unless you have kids you can't know how weak they can make someone as strong as yourself. Who else better to commiserate with than a comrade in arms who knows how the game is played?

And your best playmates hold the potential for great playdates, too. If your children and hers get along well, you can do all sorts of fun stuff together. Young and older, you each have a buddy. You can sign up for late morning mommy-and-me yoga and a healthy lunch fit for the yogi group, make appointments for side-by-side manis and pedis, settle in for story time at the library (even though the adult social time will have to be at a whisper), and share a picnic in the park and the food preparation that goes along with it.

Other Players

The wife of your husband's best friend may be a bit personality deprived. Not your choice for a girlfriend, but she's someone who plays a part in your life, and you can't do much about that. As an NM, the solution may have been simpler—just drinking that extra Cosmo when at dinner with her. When you're a PM but there are still no kids in the other couple's near future, give yourself a reprieve by inviting them over on a weekend. With your kids present and accounted for, your focus "unwillingly" will be on obliging food requests, answering interruptions, and berating them enough to ensure minimal time for true conversation with her. And when you both have kids, then you have something to talk about. It opens up the ever popular pre-school, pediatrician, and potty training conversations. Dinner becomes more bearable with all the new in-common subjects to cover.

Or does your husband have a holdout friend? You know the type, an eternal bachelor who believes marriage and kids are for other "suckers" and wants no part. More aggravating is his attempt to get your hubby to subscribe to that nonsense and employ him as a wingman. And then there's his love life: with no real intentions to make her into something else, he strings along his girlfriend of the day and wants you to "get to know her better," which wouldn't be so painful if you thought she'd be around another month. Quickly this buddy will learn how a mom like you responds to a dope like him. When he invites one of these bimbos *du jour* to dine with you, plan a barrage of questions delicately delivered for Mr. Macho. It's a stretch away from the gracious hostess a PM normally is, but it's a necessary tactic. In front of her you interrogate him with: "What was your last girlfriend's name and occupation?" (to which he answers: "I forgot and exotic dancer"), "What's your real feeling on commitment?", and "Has your mother ever met one of your girlfriends?" He'll want no part of your curious company, and you should be safe for a good six months and another six girlfriends. Her initial shock will likely be replaced by gratitude for your having let her in on his little secret and saving her from wasting her precious child-bearing years in the end.

Parents of Kids' Friends

Consider yourself blessed if you want to make lunch plans with the moms of little Sydney's classmates. Likely you won't. But for the sake of your kids, you'll inevitably have to chummy up with a mother whose sole purpose, it seems, is to annoy you. Nevertheless, you must maintain a relationship of sorts—she may have redeeming qualities that make for a good carpool partner, or maybe she's someone you trust (and your wee one will willingly go to) as an emergency contact. You'll be civil for the kids, but you won't feel a loss when your child and hers finally splinter off to different middle schools. Along the way, you will meet this kind of mom and many others, and if you haven't as yet, expect one of these to be coming soon to a town near you.

The Micro-Manager Mom ● ● •
This lady is lucky enough not to have to work, but she's made her life's work making sure her children's lives are

perfectly unblemished. She's staying at home to assure it all goes their (and her) way. The PM is way wary of this high-maintenance mom. You know there will be a phone call if your son doesn't make one hundred percent nice-nice and befriend her beloved boy. Then once they become friends and play together like true buds, she'll badger you to sign up your son for baseball instead of soccer because she wants them together forever. She may even go as far as harassing phone calls to town hall to ensure they're placed on the same team. And don't think she won't have the audacity to badmouth other kids in front of yours in hopes your son will be partial to hers.

> My instinct is to protect my children from pain. But adversity is often the thing that gives us character and backbone.
> —*Nicole Kidman*

Here's a word to the wise: never outwardly cross this particular maniacal mom. She's capable of brainwashing her kids to be just as petty and controlling as she is. Your son may get snubbed along the way if things go sour, and the wrath he'll endure is not worth your joy in telling her off. When pushed about the sports subject again, a little "forgetfulness" that made you "miss" the deadline is the best and safest excuse.

The Stalker ● ● •

She likes your kid just fine, but it's you she really wants. Not in any sexual way, but by her side. She has turned *best friend* into a verb, and her goal is *best-friending* you forever. None of the plans she wants to make have anything to do with the kids. She invites you to lunch, she asks what your weekend looks like (the evenings, that is), and drops your name around town as if the relationship has been solidified.

You don't see it working? Then stop her in her tracks at the preschool door. Your tactics should be swift and uninviting: "I'm on a diet and only eating pre-bagged foods from home," (to avoid lunches out) or "our trusted baby-sitter is indefinitely AWOL and our weekends are being spent at the homestead catching up on quality time with the kids," (to deflect her inviting herself over), and "I hear you're talking me up, that's so sweet. But I prefer my business, good or bad, remains anonymous among town folk" (giving the illusion that your family may be under the witness protection program, hopefully enough to scare her off, not intrigue her more). A Posh Mom would never intentionally be cruel, yet niceties do nothing for this one-track mom; they only lead her on and inevitably let her down.

The Carefree Mom ● ● •

Right off the bat you know this spells trouble, because no normal mom has no cares. But this one doesn't have a care to speak of. Even her children can't depend on her. She may or may not still be smoking something left over from her college days, but even if she's quit, her actions don't show it. Her kids are always late for school, she slacks off on carpool promises, and if she makes it to after-school sports, she's forgotten the uniform. Obviously this mom needs someone to pick up the tattered pieces of her agenda, but don't let it be you. If she needs transportation for her daughter to gymnastics for the fourth time in a row, oblige once more, but feign asking her to do the return trip. Once she sees the relationship requires reciprocation, it's a good bet you'll be free of her.

The MAP Mom ● ● ●

MAP stands for Mine Are Perfect, and she believes her kids are just that: beyond polite, born from the womb sugar sweet, and excel at any endeavor they even think to try. We moms all have a little bit of this syndrome (our kids are "just having fun" when they're falling all over each other at a restaurant while other mothers are "just plain rude" to allow their kids to cause such a ruckus), but the sane ones keep it in check somewhere closer to reality. This selectively blind MAP mom chooses to see all situations from her tainted point of view. Befriending her will only result in frustration and ill-will toward her and her children. Don't dare try to enlighten her about the time her son whacked yours in the back so hard you felt the vibration. You're not her offspring, so inevitably anything you say or do will turn into an "I-know-you-are-but-what-am-I" fest. You're better off yes-ing her and flashing your pearly whites from a distance. It's a much better way to keep this acquaintance.

Married with Children

You like her but he's just as nice. Your husband loves his new buddy and the wife rates high on his scale, too. And their kids' genders and ages overlap with yours. These couples handpicked by you and your husband are the friendships that usually work out and last longest. Ah, ain't life grand—until the day when the two families are all together. Their Jack knocks your Lucas on the head, with a plastic hammer, no less. Without apology from the son and no parental recognition, you're livid. Ever the Posh Mom, don't let it affect your feelings for the friendship, as hard as that may be. Parenting skills or lack thereof should not make or break the unity. Soothe your son and let her deal with hers. The next time it may be reversed (it's almost a guarantee), and you'll take the high ground and have to dispense the discipline.

If their kids are sweet (aside from an age-appropriate blow or two), that's just icing on the cake, as well as license to fill the agenda with plans for the families to frolic together. The possibilities are endless: trick or treating on Halloween, Sunday night dinner *al fresco*, a parade for the Fourth of July, or long weekend vacations out of town.

Keeping It All Together

You are surrounded by a true cast of characters—the myriad of relationships you have forged and formed as a mom. Some joined the set when they blew you away in their screen test others slipped on by way of marriage. You might be bombarded by bad behavior (kids and adults alike), persnickety attitudes (kids and adults alike), overzealous fans, ridiculous expectations, and the need to maintain your sex appeal. But ever the Posh Mom, you come through the triumphant heroine, applauding with the rest of the audience as the credits role.

Say What You Mean

Posh Mom motto # 14 encourages a PM to speak her mind, which we know oh-so-well is sometimes easier said than done.

Your kids

What you say:
"It's late. It's bath time, then bedtime. You have school tomorrow."

What you mean:
Calgon take me away! My day was grueling—you need to get into bed so I can get into a bubble bath.

Your hubby

What you say:
"Last night was amazing."

What you mean:
Certainly it was all that with him, but you're also referring to the fact your youngest slept through the night.

Your friends
What you say:
"Gotta go now, but I'll call you this afternoon."

What you mean:
Kids got me way too crazed to chat. I'll call within a week (or sooner if I can swing it).

Your parents
What you say:
"The kids really miss you."

What you mean:
We need to call in a chit from the built-in baby-sitters.

Your mother-in-law
What you say:
"Can I borrow your flower arranging expertise?"

What you mean:
Keep your nose-butting distance when I'm disciplining the kids.

Your child's teacher

What you say:

"My son is reading already. Is that something other kids in the class are doing?"

What you mean:

He's the smartest one in here, isn't he?

Chapter Four
Outer Posh

Back in the day, Taylor was considered somewhat of a "hottie" by her college mates, as well as in her own mind—and she didn't mind it one bit. In times of internal insecurity, she had come to rely on this image as sort of generator of backup power to propel her mood.

So Tuesday was a shocker. The morning light shone through her bathroom, and either the mirror was on heightened magnification and distorting things or she really did have an age spot, albeit in a stage of infancy, on her right cheek. There are certain markers of age she always promised to accept, but why couldn't this first and especially unsightly spot show up somewhere she could make it unseen—like her lower back?

A dab of concealer later, she passed her husband, who gave her a look of concern as he eyed her skirt. "Aren't you dressed up?" he quipped. Probably it was the skirt he was referring to, which may have been a little shorter than what she usually sported. But after her *unnerving experience with her reflection, she knew she needed a bandage for her ego, and she had decided to go with a little leg-lengthening one.*

Later, in the fitting room, with a fifteen-minute window before her daughter's after-school dentist appointment, she quickly threw on sixteen different tops, all of which said "teeny bopper" instead of her intended "show stopper." It was official: she was feeling the doldrums. At dinner, as everyone conversed about the day, she silently cried an "I'm getting older" tear.

The savior of the day appeared right after teeth-brushing time, as she read and rocked her six-year-old son. Just when they got to the part when the boy in the story was elated because he finally got the puppy he asked for, her son wrapped his arms around her neck. "I love you more dan any dog in the world, Mom," he gushed. With one sentence he has unwittingly put her self-esteem back in the sky-high place where it should be.

You're only a posh package if your wrapping paper says so, and the Posh Mom has impeccable style. She doesn't subscribe to motherhood as a free ticket to wardrobe shortcomings; rather, she sees it as freedom from enslavement to the sometimes outlandish dictates of high fashion magazines. She's also thankful when she remembers that there's a wide, deep moat between perfect and put-together, especially for a woman with kids.

Whenever social obligation calls, she arrives looking simply well done, never faputzed. After school or after dark, wherever she appears, she makes the most of her appearance. Her closet is hanging with the goods, and she knows just when to use them—or not (the Posh Mom would be the first to tell you that heels on the soccer field are ridiculous, not fabulous).

Never one to be caught off-guard or be off color, her highlight appointment was made for eight weeks from the date the last foil was placed. But if a raging petite posh ear infection gets in the way of the faux bits of sunshine that wind through her hair, she knows her products and can run out (after doling out the antibiotics) to buy a color-enhancing shampoo—like Pantene Pro-V Expressions—to rev up color and prevent fading. And her nails are at the very least coated in a close-to-natural shade that masks the chips she wears as her badge of motherhood.

It takes instinct, effort, and homework (magazines no textbooks are fundamental) to stay ahead in her internal battle to remain outwardly sensational, but the pressure is eased by the fact that no mom is all that all the time. She's just hanging on tight to keep her blow-dry above water and to the cliché but factual vainglorious words of wisdom: when you look good, you feel good.

Yet, like the true icon she is, the Posh Mom figured out how to make it look effortless when it was anything but. Recognizing and admitting that life as she knew it as an NM was over stopped her from getting left in la-la land. Dealing with that reality meant taking action against the obstacles in the way of becoming a put-together mom. Whether it is hitting her treadmill after the kids go to bed or keeping a promise to her best friend to grab lunch and go for a quick shoe shop once a month, she squeezes in time for herself and makes no apologies for it. And why should she?

You know who she is. She's not necessarily a beauty, but you have to admit, she's got it going on. It's always the same: The second she walks into the room, everyone takes notice. In a quick once-over you check out her bag (the one you're on the waitlist for), envy her of-the-moment shoes, sneak peeks at her smoothed hair, and to top it off, marvel at her fantastic outfit—again. Here's how you can be her, too.

Fashion for the Mommy Set

Clothing is a priority that ranks high on the "she's all that" scale. Back in the day, having kids sent moms on a sort of style-sabbatical. Who needed to be up on fashion codes when feeding, bathing, and caring for little ones was the only name of the mommy game? Great ensembles would only sit in her closet because she always put on clothing durable enough to hang out with her kids and possibly with the neighbor's children if they came a' calling. An apron was a necessity; a great pair of jeans was not.

Now a mom always has somewhere she needs to be, and peers expect her to look the posh part. Cohorts are not generous with free passes to stay home and look homely, and neither are their behind-your-back whispers. And it starts immediately. Music, yoga, and gym classes are created especially for babies fresh out of the womb, and you need something to wear to all these events. A more experienced mom's schedule is jam-packed too, whether it's a school fund-raiser, lunch with a colleague, or book club with her posh posse—and she can't wear tracksuits every day.

> She was the archetypal selfless mother: living only for her children, sheltering them from consequences of their actions, and in the end doing them irreparable harm.
> —*Marcia Muller*

Whoa, Nellie, you say. Before we slam the closet door, you want us to know that it's not a complete waste case in there—there are some cotton-with-just-the-right-amount-of-Lycra outfits from the baby-in-the-belly days you're still perfectly comfortable in. And you held on to some of your fave NM ditties.

Not so fast, Poshie. For starters, you'll soon be slimming out of those sleek but clearly made for belly-hiding frocks, despite how stylish they may have been. But more important, you're a PM now, no longer an NM—you need to tweak your look so you don't give off the air of a no-kids wannabe, an abhorrent path to take.

So donate only-for-NM-pieces and pack up any maternity items to hand down to your sister or best gal pal (whoever's on deck) ASAP—you need to get out of those outfits while you still can, before you get so comfy in them that you're refreshing your wardrobe at A Pea in the Pod. Then, hit a spot like Old Navy to get some inexpensive in-between stretch-waist pants to hold you over until you're no longer busting out of your former size.

But outfitting a fashionista is no longer the cinch it was when the PM was the NM. Back then, all those extra hours for browsing and shopping, plus her basic instinct for panache, made every season an exciting mission to seek out the best of the offerings. Now, when she's on a quest for orange juice with no pulp and the brand of mac and cheese with that certain special-shaped pasta, expeditions for shoes and bags get chucked out the window. In fact, we're frequenting the one windowless fluorescent-lit store there is: the supermarket—and trips there sometimes number a ridiculous three times a week.

Poshmom.com Pick

A Posh Mom sees her inner self as just as important as her outer self, and this goes for her inner garments as well as for her inner being. Our best undercover friend for helping out in that department is Spanx. Their Hide and Seek cami works wonders on belly bulge that may have everything—or nothing—to do with pregnancy.

Just because you're feverishly tracking down nutritional (and some nutritionless) favorites for your household, though, you can't ignore the fact that your stylish soul needs to be fed. Your most necessary fuel? You've heard it before—the magazines. With your busy lineup, trying to buy of-the-moment pieces and put together looks from scratch can turn out messy (you know those hide-their-faces *Glamour* don'ts...). Copying, while always frowned upon at school, is legal in this arena, and several sources make this easier, including buying guides in the back of magazines with feature pages that mix and match for you, catalogs in which stylists have already put together the well-thought-out outfit, and good ol' online shopping. Your best bet is to hone the info from the dedicated fashion editors who sat front row at the hottest fashion shows and translate the trends to work in your town. Delivered straight to your door, the glossies are your ultimate Cliff's Notes. Subscribe to two minimum, and don't go on an environmental kick to save trees by canceling subscriptions if they wind up unread, adorning your coffee table. You'll eventually find a few minutes to flip through. Try putting them in the car to keep you perfectly content when baseball practice runs fifteen minutes late. And if you can spare the room, store them—at least for the season.

Wardrobe Basics ● ● ●

The discriminating Posh Mom can best get a handle on

a wardrobe that's similar to her kids' after-school activity list: not so big as to overwhelm her. With less extraneous pieces staring back at you, you hone in on outfits that are piping-hot posh, like a great pair of of-the-moment jeans, the belt that makes a splash across a monochromatic outfit, or a patterned top in this season's hot print (whether argyle, stripes, or Pucci-inspired).

Fit to a tee

Admit it, what you wear most is the low (though not lowly) garment on the fashion totem pole: it's the tee. Long-sleeved, short-sleeved, or no sleeves at all, printed or plain, the tee is the hip mom's uniform and very of the moment at the moment. Comfy and cotton, able to be thrown in the machine for severe stain removal, the all-purpose tee can be dressed up or down depending on what it's debuting with. Stock up on cheapies in black, white, gray, and a few in the season's palette. Since they don't make a very big dent in the cash flow, you won't think twice about pruning your closet of the faded and frayed ones. The bonus: keeping the essentials inexpensive also keeps your wallet cocked for a splurge on a handful of extra-soft, cut-to-perfection designer tees, even if they are destined for a short life span. Put tees with any of the essential "now" bottoms (be it skater shorts or capris) and voilà! Look cute and play hard so you don't have to play it safe and deny your kids the messy joys of childhood like muddy puddles and blue cotton candy.

Posh Picks: The Poshest T-shirt

The best-feeling tees are the combed cotton ones from Peru, as opposed to their rougher cotton counterparts made in Cambodia. The best-looking ones are blended with other fibers so they hug in all the right places. As for the best design, you don't want them gaudy, but you do want them to have enough character to give them that je ne sais quoi that allows you to wear them out and about in all good fashion conscience.

Time-Alone Tees
No trips to the pottery-making place in these babies. Wear them only at posher outings such as a school concert, work (under a fitted blazer), or a lunch to honor a friend.
 1. Theory
 2. James Perse
 3. C & C
 4. Three Dot
 5. Petit Bateau

Fun Tees
For everything from casual get-togethers to walks around town.
 1. Splendid

2. Trunk, Ltd.
3. Michael Stars
4. Banana Republic

Down and Dirty
Inexpensive enough to wear for backyard baseball—and can be used as a dust cloth after a season's worth of washing.
1. Old Navy Tiny Tees
2. Gap Perfect Fit
3. Vintage tee line from Target

The rest of the body

But a T-shirt, as cute as it may be, doesn't stand alone unless you're going to bed. You need to pair it with essentials for your bottom, like jeans fit with the leg style of the season, be it boot, straight, or skinny. Make sure you're flush with lots of shades and washes so you're ready for day or night. Khakis are understudy to the hotter than hot jean—don't bring out the old preppy pleated ones with no shape to speak of, but do find the low-waisted cargo version or a pair that's snug enough to show your hips are anything but manly.

Day Rules ● ● ●

Whether working, working out, or working with her kids on a sand castle, the Posh Mom dresses task specific, and she never blurs the lines. Out and about in workout clothes is only good until noon. Once the clock strikes p.m., people will assume (and rightly so, no?) you haven't showered and have no plan to. And contrary to what you might see at the local mall, you absolutely cannot pair workout clothes with anything other than sneakers. No tattered shoes, ripped jeans (even when they are in style, for moms they always need to be archived), or see-through shirts. And no dressing like a teen queen: It's great when our faces and bodies look young enough to be mistaken for the baby-sitter; it's not okay to look like you've poached from her closet. Don't forget that your "private parts" need fashion sense, too. Never sport a panty line, always wear good underwear (you may find yourself in a hospital or communal fitting room, hopefully the latter), and never let them see your bra strap, La Perla or not.

In the confines of home, comfy clothes are one thing, but a convoluted concoction is bad for the ego—yours and his. No matter the memories his old sweats from college conjure up, frame them, don't wear them. The effort to pull on a potato sack sweatshirt is the same as to zip into a fitted hoodie. Equally cozy but unequalled in style, the oversized frock has you looking more like his college roommate than his pretty posh wife. Which would you prefer?

Nighttime Fun ● ● •

Let's face it: these days, nights out are fewer and farther between, courtesy of your eager-to-get-the-day-started-at-dawn team. When you get a precious chance, seize the opportunity to strut your sense of fashion that's squelched in daylight hours. But make the important distinction between "fancy" and "decked out." The former is stuffy and from your grandmother's era (bless her soul), while the latter says trendy, cool, and confident. You know the difference: she used to wear nylons when the temperature dipped, now the protocol is bare-legged and shivering. Her shawl was about needlework and awful pastels, but today's luxe wrap, puts you at your style peak—even if the clothes underneath don't deserve a sneak peak.

The sleeveless, sequined top that's too over the top for lunch with the girls makes a proper debut at your neighbors' dinner party. And date night with your man is just the night to stuff into the push-up bra and pull out the clothes you wore when you were a married NM. In the later hours, there is no need to apologize for form-fitting (never skin-tight) outfits that flaunt your posh assets. After dusk, even breasts whose daytime deed is to nourish your newborn have license to spill over a cleavage-baring top.

Accessory Necessities ● ● •

An unaccessorized Posh Mom may as well be a naked one. To her, an outfit is much like a chocolate soufflé:

both need all the ingredients to be perfect (just raw egg and flour is dry and can even be dangerous—think salmonella)! If neutral in color, basics like belts, shoes, and scarves will work with anything. The trick is to plot out the ultimate get-up the night before, when no one is awake to interfere with the creativity. The morn brings breakfast prep and three different menu requests from one little person and is not the time to think about a well put-together ensemble. In fact, the distraction could drive you right into heels with a too-short skirt—a surefire way to look like a lady of the nightmare.

Indulging in a few pieces that are worth their single-use status is mandatory. You know what we're talking about—that pair of fuchsia Manolos you stepped up to the plate for and now proudly own. They won't be worn to many karate class demonstrations, but where you do go with them you're assured of fetching compliments. Just don't put them on at the same time as your new rhinestoned jeans—pulling out all your closet's bells and whistles at once takes you from understated to overdone. You just need one brilliant extra mixed with the ordinary to stand out. Think of Jackie-O shades: they turn a white button down and jeans from hang-around-the-house to hang-out-on-the-Riviera.

Like the rest of your wardrobe, do a changing of the guard each season for your accessories. If you live in perpetual warmth, pare down on hats and scarves (you still need a good Hermes silk one for belting) and go heavy on sunglasses, sun hats, and bathing suit cover-ups (The last

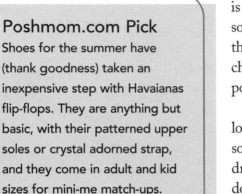

Poshmom.com Pick

Shoes for the summer have (thank goodness) taken an inexpensive step with Havaianas flip-flops. They are anything but basic, with their patterned upper soles or crystal adorned strap, and they come in adult and kid sizes for mini-me match-ups.

is especially indispensable so that you don't do the thunder thigh jiggle as you chase your kids around the pool or beach.)

In cold-weather locales, looking good in winter can sometimes seem like a pipe dream, since stylish and down-filled are often contradictory. But this is survival of the poshest, and you need to prepare for living with the elements. Buy a set of gargantuan waterproof gloves, a polar-fleece scarf, and a warm knit cap to keep your ears toasty (even if it makes you look like a burglar or mercilessly destroys your hairdo)—you'll be glad you did when you're out sledding with your family. Then invest in soft leather gloves, a cashmere scarf, and a hat that goes gentle on your hair for the quick walk from parking lot to fancy restaurant.

And it rains everywhere, so be chic when it pours. A Burberry rain hat (the Brits' contribution to stylish waterproofing) and streamlined rain boots are classics and more refined than a coat thrown over your head and tattered running shoes.

Baubles transcend the seasons if they're genuine—anywhere, anytime you can count on diamonds (or sapphires or gold or pearls) to be your best friend. Costume jewelry, however, as funky and fun as a piece may be, is undoubtedly season-specific and may even have a shelf life. A delicate Swarovski crystal in the palest jewel tone may need to hibernate for the winter, and a chunky metal medallion that was all the rage this summer will leave you looking like you got left back a year when the next spring's lines are showing wispy chains and understated charms.

The Price of Accessorizing

A Posh Mom heeds the accessory calling but doesn't always answer with highfalutin' or pricey pieces.

Fancy
Mikimoto pearls

Budget
Your depression-era grandmother's much less expensive but much more epic heirloom strands

---

Fancy
Dolce & Gabbana leopard-print belt

Budget
No-name leopard-print scarf woven through belt loops

Fancy
Rachel Weisman headband

Budget
Pucci inspired number from Claire's

Fancy
Fendi leather bag

Budget
A consignment store find of an out-dated but you-make-it-make-a-comeback-and-become-chic-vintage style

---

Fancy
Tracey Zabar charm bracelet

Budget
A teen store knockoff that can be knocked around

Fancy
Oliver Peoples "Commander" aviator sunglasses

Budget
Eighties-inspired metal framed shades from the mall kiosk

Fancy
The Blackberry Pearl

Budget
A leftover but still functioning Palm Pilot rescued from your office's recycle pool (or from your hubby's)

Fancy
Earth-tone flip flops with a tiny silver Prada buckle

Budget
Multiple pairs from Old Navy in all shades of brown.

Fancy
A yellow Canary diamond from Tiffany

Budget
A yellow citrine from Zales

Organizing the Closet

If you are to have any success at your intention of lickety-split outfitting, you must take seriously the ritual of clearing and organizing your closet. When it's time to dress (while simultaneously dressing your kids), the decision about what to wear becomes infinitely easier when all components are in full view and easily accessible. Sectioning your pants and shirts by color and by season is a good start. Shoe racks instead of floor piles are chaos-free (since the rest of your life has its fill) and less of an invitation for your daughter's dress-up shows. To prevent an avalanche of tees off the shelf, go three deep max and segregate your work-out from your go-to-work ones (the unpaid home job or the office kind). Like two-year-olds, socks and panties can't share—don't try to make them. Tiny as your thongs may be, they can get lost in a sea of socks that—think about it—even though they are Downy fresh, hang out in sweaty shoes all day. Yuck! Just keep them in separate drawers.

Your closet has some staying power (unlike your kids' closets, which are like revolving doors due to size changes), and no one is going through your things to tell you what no longer fits your waist or fits your life. You need to self-purge (preferably four times a year) so you're not stuck wading through hangers full of outdated styles and overused outfits.

What's In, What's Out ● ● ●

Parting is sweet sorrow for classics that were supposed to last forever (or at least a long while). Yes, you spent a bundle on that cashmere cardigan, but the small balls of nap that have formed what seems like a cement-infused attachment that even your trusty piller can't remove make it necessary to bid it a tearful good-bye. Weed out former favorites that are now wasted space-takers or garments whose labels said washable but never mentioned that water immersion changes the size from medium to itty-bitty (sometimes we really can blame shrinkage!).

And there's no room for anything in your closet that says "posh girl"—you're now part of the elite class of Posh Mom. Gift the belly-baring tees to your neighbor's seventeen-year-old daughter and toss the pants that give you plumber's butt when you bend to pick up your son. Keep a few pieces you just can't part with: ten years from now (the average life of a fashion cycle) they may make a return and you can dust them off then if you still feel the need.

You can also allow a few not-fit-to-wear-in-public things to remain, because they are just what you need for the finger-painting you were cajoled into with the kids. Still, put a self-imposed limit on how many "smocks" get to stay. The majority of your outfits should be in good-enough shape to be worn outside your own home, which rules out all those that are faded, stretched, and "a tad too tight."

On the flip-side, if your children are younger, there's no room on your racks for too many outfits designated as delicate, because they have the potential to interfere with mothering. If the protection of your clothes takes precedence over the good of your children—hello...get your mind out of *Vogue*, that's just not the page you're on now. Odds are you'll get wrinkled, stained, or ruined by day's end, and with the stress-inducing price tag off but not forgotten, it can't be taken lightly. Yet, what fashionable woman doesn't have to have that buttery suede shirt, even if it can't be worn around little hands? A few pricey lusts are musts for times you are flying solo. But when you're home, practicality must reign.

You're a sucker (hate to be the bearer of the news) if: you suck in to fit into your once best-fitting jeans, hold it 'til ten to zip your cutest black cocktail number, and breathe out in short spurts that simulate childbirth techniques once you've wriggled into that sexy spaghetti strap number with body hugging Lycra. Understandable, yes, but not tolerated for the Posh Mom. The khakis that don't even pretend to come close to buttoning because you're only eight months postpartum need to be put on closet-rest even if you thought they'd be back in action by now. Pay tribute to them and all other items in the back of your closet that might have another shot. Don't forget about these items—check them out periodically, but make sure they are ready for the limelight before reintroduction to the social scene.

And spend no time debating what flattered your once plumped-up-from-pregnancy-hormones figure. You know what we're talking about—the sexy, strappy number meant for a well-endowed friend that you bought while breast-feeding, completely disregarding the laws of nature that would soon shrivel you back to your pre-nursing bra size. Yes, it can be painful to part with clothes that once made you look amazing, but rest assured you are aesthetically in a better place now.

Have you chosen the hardest profession that pays not a cent? Conservative pinstripes and tailored suits from NM days will never be worn for your hard work at home, so send them to your former colleague with love. Break the silky ties with extracurricular clothes that no that no longer fit your lifestyle, either. Snow pants from your single skiing days, no matter how cute you look in them, are nothing but a cool blast from your past when your honey and kids prefer the beach to the slopes. Follow this rule: If you have to invent an imaginary event for any outfit, it needs to go.

Take a Trip to the Tailor ● ● •

While you're weeding out, separate what's worthless from what's just shy of perfect. If your closet has a full-size mirror, transform the area into a changing room. Anything one full size too small or a size too large (a good problem!), gets sent packing. Even the most skilled needle and thread can't change a size that drastically—

with any success. Either a friend, Goodwill, or dress-up for your daughter is a worthy cause for donation.

Rescue anything from the grab bag that makes you look svelte, though. It's a keeper. The rush of positive body image tingles are worth whatever the hassle or price to fix such garments. Don't be too hasty if your next try-on leaves you feeling like you're tipping the scales. A little let-out in the waist of those pants that have you breathing from your nose rather than your diaphragm is nothing a good seamstress can't handle. She's worth searching for and paying for her services is money well spent.

A Posh Mom trusts her instincts on such important matters but relies on the experienced words of her friends, too. (Always get recommendations—*gawd forbid* the hem on your unbelievable black pants with a price tag to match winds up too short.) And a PM's so shrewd, she'd never be vulnerable to a "closed" sign with nowhere to turn—a second choice plugged into her PDA is imperative for those times when she needs a quick turnaround. Add high-quality dry cleaners to the list of professionals, too. They work miracles on stains, like the fruit punch your son "shared" with your crisp white button-down.

Shopping 101

The Posh Mom loves to shop. Even if it's just stolen moments between preschool pick-ups and little league carpool, she takes guiltless pleasure in her trade. The secret to success? She's wickedly honest, refusing to trick herself into believing her body is something it's not. Whether the body she inhabits today is her dream one or it's still in the works, she's shopping for the reflection in the mirror. If five months post-birth there's still extra junk in the trunk, she vows to stop secretly shoveling in the Tootsie Rolls from the kids' goody bags while still accepting her new size in pants. She stands by her convictions, which are the same when shopping at the market: never shop when hungry or menstruating—the decisions will be disastrous with a mood to match.

Shop, Drop, and Roll ● • •
A Posh Mom's popularity keeps her on the A-list of diverse events and she never wants to be caught with her pants down—at the very least, not the wrong ones. Keep ahead of the invites and your less-than-open shopping schedule—one or two outstanding dressy outfits need to be secured and tailored at the beginning of each season. At least one shopping score should be a dress (which by virtue of being one piece eases last-minute indecisiveness when you're under the gun and forgot that you promised Aunt Joan you'd definitely make her anniversary dinner at the new French bistro across town). Getting a handle on more formal wear is not as easy. Dinner parties, shows (Broadway or ballet recital), and holidays may have you

on a mad search. You can dream of occasion-specific shopping (and it is recommended), but it's not always possible. One look at your unibrow this morning and you know the hour you set aside between religious school drop-off and pick-up needs to be spent with your wax lady, not running to get a dress. So, Thursday turns into Friday. But Friday may not be as fruitful as you expected, which means Saturday will require a squeezed-in shopping jaunt after soccer. Then, if the pants your butt looked best in need a hem, you'll be forced to continue searching and possibly walk away with something not quite as uplifting but the right length.

Worst case scenario, if it's an hour before your reservation and you're standing perplexed and naked in front of your mirror, don't panic. You're bound to have a friend who's a similar size (note to self: if you don't have one, make one). The hallmark of a good friend is being able to call last-minute, enter her closet with complete carte blanche to take anything you see fit (and that fits) to get you to the event on time. If she's not home and you don't have a key (note to self again: get one), go to a tried-and-true outfit, it'll never let you down. And forget the nagging feeling that you've already worn it out with this crowd, likely they can't remember what appetizer they just ordered, let alone your fancy pants.

Q&A: Jara's Dance-a-thon

The situation:
As soon as I stepped out of the shower this morning I remembered tonight was my little girl's ballet recital. Could have been the sight of her posed in first position and clad in a tutu and backward leotard on the bath mat that flicked my memory chip, but I'd like to attribute my recollection to a clear and well-oiled thought process that keeps my schedule in check. Too bad my gray stuff was a little squeaky later that afternoon when I was running errands galore, zooming home to prep dinner, give homework ultimatums, and draw baths. When my daughter asked, "Do I need a bath before I go on stage?" it was like a ton of tiny ballet slippers falling on my head. I could fudge to her the fact that I forgot, but not to myself. With no thought of what to wear, certainly no time to shop, and hair that had been pulled into a cute but plastered-tight pony all day, what to do?

The solution:
Damage control. Step one: I assessed the situation. It's an early evening event, cool jeans or even trendy-cut khakis will do. Deep breath—ever the Posh Mom, I have a stash in my closet to draw from.

Phew. I paired them with a pricey T-shirt I'd wear out, not out and about. A belt and shoe with a tiny heel added polish and brought it all home—or to the auditorium. Step two: Take stock and refresh. Did a re-do on that hanging low pony that I was traipsing around in all day, then gathered it into a loose knot that's equally fab but not the same day 'do other proud mothers may have seen me in earlier. Then slicked lips with a little more shine. Step three: Leave no equipment behind. I grabbed the camera-charger (I can find a socket anywhere), had hubby pick up a bouquet of roses for our ballerina, and I looked like I'd been plotting all day.

Boutique or Bargain-Basement? ● ● •

Nothing is wrong with the buy-and-return-shopping style of the picky PM who is always having to rush her decisions (those orange slingbacks straight from the runway don't translate so well onto playroom floors). But it only works if the store's policy is lenient. She needs to stick with well-known retail chains whose rules give her plenty of time to ponder, rather than penalizing her feminine bouts of indecisiveness. Boutiques that bring out the more intimate relationship between salesgirl and buyer usually offer up rarer finds, but small boutiques are also less likely to let minor lapses go unpunished. You may be quickly caught in the midst of bitter return sessions, leaving you walking out with store credit in hand and (undue but real) anger toward the lady at the register. It's actually your fault, of course, thinking eight days is close enough to their one week window during which when they'll refund the cash.

You vow not to feel cheated because you'll use the credit, but you know that means you can't lose it first (it's been known to happen). Those little slips can be elusive just when you need them, even more so when little fingers tend to use your real wallet for pretend purchases. Make sure to take the credit slip out of your bag—even start a folder for filing all your credits and list the expiration dates clearly on the outside. When you're in "lockdown" shopping mode from the move into the lovely but costly "new construction," this file of unbought treasures will brighten your day and freshen your closet.

Online Finds ● ● ●

The Internet has become suburban Poshie's best new friend. Clicks away from the fashion pulse, she keeps up with City Posh and then some. You can get your fix any night of the week, even when the shopping trip had to reluctantly be crossed off today's list. The only negatives are not feeling fabrics and no fitting room. Buyer beware: It's a trip to the P.O. (everything invariably goes back on that "to-do" list) if one site's idea of "medium" turns out to mean "extra small."

On the Prowl ● ● •

Visiting favorite haunts and discovering new stores qualifies as providing out-and-about activity for your little ones and retail therapy for yourself, a doubly happy whammy. Participate in this ritual as frequently as their small amounts of patience allow, but don't attempt an actual purchase. These trips are research expeditions only, unless it's socks you seek. There's a big learning curve we suffer through with this rule, because we foolishly believe and continually attempt to buy with kids at our side. Did the flying mannequin or its rolling head not clue you in? If that didn't clinch it, think of the fuchsia Empire-waist shirt that makes you look like you're in your fifth month when you're really at your skinniest. A closer inspection of your closet reveals that all errant buys like that took place while little ones were present.

Posh Picks: Best Shopping for Mom on the Web

1. Shopbop.com
2. Eluxury.com
3. Shopintuition.com
4. Singer22.com
5. Revivalboutique.com
6. Bluefly.com
7. Gap.com
8. Bigdropnyc.com
9. Lisakline.com
10. Bluebee.com
11. Shopbluegenes.com
12 Yoox.com
13. Shopemilygrace.com
14. tg170.com
15. Shopkitson.com

Copying Is the Sincerest Form of Flattery ● ● •

Although a Posh Mom would like to be seen as the discoverer of all things fashionable, sometimes you have to outsource. Admiring other Posh Moms and prying well-kept shopping secrets from their tight lips can be very fruitful, if you succeed. Be subtle and use flattery. Compliment the neckline of her tee, the thinning effect of her jeans, then coyly slip in, "Where did you find them?" It's a one-two punch. It's hard for even the stingiest women to fib when flattered and questioned face to face. But never ask how much she paid—that's amateurish and always out of the question.

As a Posh Mom, you, too, will find yourself squinting under the interrogation lamp. A good friend to the core, lead your close circle directly to the source, and even provide an introduction to the salesgirl. For curious acquaintances, try to mix it up with pat and practiced answers before divulging. Never rude, always polite, offer up only, "It was a gift, isn't it great?" or "I've had it for so long, I can't even remember."

Mirror, Mirror on the Wall ● ● •

The Posh Mom isn't fooled by the mirror in the dressing room (it was manufactured to err toward skinny) or by the salesperson fawning over every single thing she tries on. She is notorious for instant gratification, but before clipping tags, the PM gets to the safety of home to re-try purchases. The hip sales chick who is mother only to a ferret can't possibly work her pressure from miles away and the PM gets good old honesty from her kids, just about the only people she can count on for no-holds-barred feedback. Their comments may be brutal but surprisingly on the mark. "You look like an astronaut" may send the smart PM running to return the hat she had a nagging inkling was too bulbous.

Fending Off Fads ● ● •

A specialty of the Posh Mom is knowing when to participate or refrain from a fad, even when it's a style she may like. Yes, stiletto heels add height and are runway-chic, but on mommy at back-to-school night, they are going to draw unwanted attention from ballet-flat clad PTA members—and their husbands. So no can do, as much as she wants the extra inches.

Spending and Sales ● ● •

For the quickness and ease that paying retail affords, a PM is willing to close her eyes and plunk down the Visa, but she's shrewd enough not to purchase an entire season's picks that way. Admittedly, last season's classics aren't as exciting anymore, but they are reliable, and revived when worn with a few new wallet-breaking ditties, like a belt with a fabulous buckle that can spruce up old-faithful jeans by day or a plain black v-neck by night. The PM works it like only she can (she holds her head up high; just cause it's old it's nothing to be ashamed of), then sits tight for the sales: it's her chance to pick up what she's been pining over and to have the thrill of spending less for it.

That said, the PM doesn't expect sale shopping to come easy, it requires discipline and diligence and the patience of a saint. It's difficult to justify giving calmness to garment acquisition when she can't always muster up that same saint-like attitude for the little ones. But, after all, this patience is for a brief stint at the store and not for an entire bath-giving episode. She pencils the start date into her planner and, before the big day hits, she befriends a salesperson who's in sync with her style. The savvy PM asks the salesperson to call when those great sandals or

> **Posh Picks:**
> **Best Shopping for**
> **Petite Posh on the Web**
> 1. Gap.com
> 2. Trendytogs.com
> 3. Crew cuts (j.crew.com)
> 4. Lifesizekids.com
> 5. Prissypoofs.com
>   (for little angels)
> 6. Bodenusa.com
> 7. Tuesdayschild.com
> 8. Piperlime.com
> 9. Natalieandfriends.com
> 10. Upandriding.com

the boys' bathing suits get marked down. This works especially well for the PM when employees are on commission.

She buddies up to a motivated salesperson who recently confided to Poshie about college debt and who would stash a stack of size 28 pants that may be just right for her new PM client.

PMs are never shortsighted; they remember salespeople at the holidays—a small investment in a high-end bath and body brand, like Judith Jackson bath salts, will go a long way toward her remembering to tell that PM about their winter sale. PMs will wrap up these gifts in anything silvery and festive (but not in the scraps from what she wrapped her kids' presents in) and then makes a special trip to drop it off so the salesperson doesn't think it was just an addendum to an already planned shopping event.

The Urge to Splurge ● ● ●

Splurging is bliss to the Posh Mom. And everyone should experience the feeling, no matter her tax bracket. In this fantasy-like world, full price is not off-limits. In fact, it is suggested. But a splurge by definition is a treat, so do it right. Indulging in a pricey lace camisole that only partially peers from your sweater's neckline is a sinful move—a popular chain store most likely carries its less costly twin. Spending it all, however, on an everyday (not to be confused with ordinary) bag can only be viewed as wise, since it's always by your side. And going overboard for the little ones—your offspring and/or any nieces and nephews with fashioned-impaired parents—is not only acceptable but obligatory. Early fashion educa tion is a stepping stone to an entire lifetime filled with appreciation for style.

Petite Posh Pickups ● • •

They are mini but that doesn't mean their looks don't matter. To a PM, her kid's style is a reflection of her own. Just as her wardrobe needs to go from drop off to drop in to see a postpartum pal, theirs needs to go from school days to after-school activities. The trick for shopping savvy for the smaller set is to do it in advance, way in advance, while pickings are still plentiful in all sizes. We're talking about shopping for spring even if you still need to whip off winter gloves to fondle the fabric. Plus, early birds are poised to get the leftover season's worms— scan the store for a sign with your favorite four-letter word to start stocking up for less for next year in their next size. But if they are picky about what they're wear- ing now—your son has to look like he's a skateboarder for profit and your daughter will only leave the house in short flouncy skirts no matter the below freezing temps—imagine the attitude 365 days from now. Reluctantly recoil the credit card if you find anything other than the basics.

Grooming Posh

Thanks to those crack-of-dawn alarm clocks she gave birth to, Poshie's time should be plentiful for readying in the a.m. So why does it always seem that she is jockeying for an intimate moment with the mirror and a blow-dryer? A runny nose has her Miss Independent acting the part of Miss Clingy, her son's backpack gets unpacked just as she hears the squeak of the school bus brakes, and a fight breaks out over control of her cell phone. The result? No time, a head full of frizz, unblended blemish zapping cream, and unconcealed under-eye circles. A plain mom might leave the house sporting all that, but a Posh Mom never would. She manages to foil her kids' plot (at some level they must know, right?) to have her spend the day tousled: she wakes up fifteen minutes early to take care of business, or she becomes the master of the perfect pony-tail. She knows it's worth a little sleep deprivation to keep looking her best. The bonus: a few minutes of never-to-be-scored-again-today solitude.

Another bonus: a lack of ill will. Relying on experi-ence, the astute PM prepares for a day that may be packed with all sorts of unwelcome surprises by sprucing herself up first so she doesn't fall into a funk because of an uncouth or unkempt state. And when someone else takes notice, their compliment is like the magic erase knob on her child's Magna-Doodle, obliterating crummy moments in an empowering instant. Besides, if you dash out of the house not at your finest (without even a swipe of lip gloss), it never fails—turn the corner in the market and you will spot the ultimate Posh Mom you just met the other day.

There's no denying the mileage you get from extra minutes spent primping, as vain as the phrase rings. A PM can only expect just so long a stretch of young smooth skin, but still there is perk-up power in little details, especially for a twenty-four hour span when the whining is nonstop, you get rear-ended on a just-fixed bumper, and your son is on the losing soccer team. When you're picking up a prescription for your little one's cough, mosey over to the makeup aisle to pick up a prescription to bring out the green in your hazel eyes. Time for you doesn't always translate into time away from them; for example, let the kids help smear on a ten-minute masque—anything goopy attracts girls and boys alike. They'll be giddy and you'll be getting gorgeous.

> My mother was the most beautiful woman I ever saw. All I am I owe to my mother. I attribute all my success in life to the moral, intellectual, and physical education I received from her.
> —George Washington

Hair, Posh Style ● • •

The Posh Mom never has a bad hair day—or at least no one would ever know if it started that way. The difference between Posh and not is that while they both may wake with problems, the Posh Mom perfects the balance between patience and control—enlisting the same mothering skills she works daily. Sure, nothing makes her smile more than sunshine and zero humidity, it means less time in front of the mirror and more time at play (with kids or possibly at a shoe sale). But when there's a moisture-filled forecast, she deals with locks that are mean and moody. A few extra minutes and a dime-sized dollop of product can put an end to any hissy fit that frizz or flatness tries to pull on her.

Like most things in life, the PMs hair came easier when she was south of thirty. Now she not only dukes it out daily with what she cursed her parents for passing on (e.g., curly Posh still wants to be stick-straight Posh and vice versa) but she also goes up against pregnancy hormones (they wreak havoc), aging follicles (yes, it's happening), and even the environment. All that means that previously tameable tresses undergo a personality transformation, leaving the PM with uncharted waters to navigate. But the PM doesn't throw in her just-out-of-the-shower turban. She researches her new 'do. She books the next available appointment with her stylist (straight hair turned kinky does qualify as an emergency, so she insists the receptionist squeezes her in). And she consults any posh pals with the same hair type—but only those she thinks have it mastered—for secret weapons to win the fight.

The right products

The Posh Mom prides herself on product knowledge and loves to share her latest finds with friends. She comes by her expertise honestly—she's a self-admitted junkie with the packed bathroom shelves to prove it. She repeatedly promises to cut herself off, but she finds it hard not to fall off the wagon when faced with a yummy-smelling shampoo or the latest spray-on shine the salesgirl promises will leave her locks looking like glass. She applies product meant only for her hair type (but can advise about all others) and sniffs out those made with natural ingredients (any time she can cut chemicals, she does). She favors companies with "no-animal testing" policies and those that use recycled materials for packaging—score one for posh social action and for her kids' futures. And she teaches her little ones early on the pleasure of products: Shampoos and sprays made just for them get rid

> ### Poshmom.com Pick
> Add one more necessary wipe to your bag—just one more thing for the aching shoulder—but luckily, it weighs next to nothing. Cutex makes an individual pouch that houses a pad for removing the manicure that went beyond chips and onto disastrous.

of knots and tangles that could be cause of much pain and suffering (for both mom and kids).

The product-savvy PM dishes with her stylist, talks to her posse, and doesn't discount the beauty aisles at her local drug store. The Posh Mom is not embarrassed to admit that some of her greatest product success stories began there. And since product discovery does not require a fitting room, it's easy shopping with kids in tow.

Beware the power of pretty packaging. It seduces you into spending more than the product inside may actually be worth. Sure, your bathroom would benefit from a display of sleek spa bottles, jars, and tubs, so do buy a few for front-row placement. Fill in behind with just-as-worthy cheapie finds.

Tools of the trade

A PM never underestimates the worthiness of her brush. Or her comb, or her iron, and she's especially protective of her blow-dryer. She's no power monger, but she knows that these are the U.N. of hair tactics, negotiating turning her bed-head into head turning every day. She believes firmly in garnering wisdom from past generations, so passing beauty know-how on to her daughter is a no-brainer; in fact, the PM regards it as her duty. Still, she lets mini posh look, though not necessarily touch. You can't take the chance that tools taken away for fluffing her kitty cat's fur might never be seen again.

Make-up, Not Made-up ● ● •

Eyes, lips, cheeks—action!
Cosmetics are a girl's best friend. The biggest mistake
non-Poshies make is underestimating the power of these
powders, creams, and pencils, and the importance of fitting in time to apply them. An extra stretch of sixty secs
in the morning is a luxury, but one you can't afford not to
cash in on. Your outfit may be of-the-moment but if your
skin is sallow and lips dull and unlined, then you missed
the mark. Skimping here is simpleton thinking and not
the surefire system of a Posh Mom—she realizes the
workload is selective and the payoff is too great. No long
regimens of piling it on: Shimmering lips (five seconds),
bronzing powder (thirty seconds), and ultra-long lashes
(a minute tops), are one hundred percent called for and
the least she can do for her appearance.

Painting it on
The right shades are crucial to your makeup bag. Fill it
with foundations, bronzers, shadows, glosses, liners, and
mascara that mesh with your skin, eyes, lips, and hair.
Choosing colors for foundation, liner, or lipstick is not
rocket science, contrary to the rantings salesgirls subject
you to at the cosmetic counter. Think natural not
painted, and take the pressure off. So your idea of dolled
up by day is jeans and a tee? What to do? Simple. A little color on your apples, some luminescence to deflect

any under-eye circles, spot swipes of concealer for stress-born blemishes, and shine for your lips. So you're off to cocktails tonight? Do kick up the color but don't go vampish—a Posh Mom favors subtlety to define her pretty assets. Visible lines on your face, just like your backside, are very bad news, so make sure the color (and your application) blends without a trace.

Foundation dos

Use foundation to even out skin tone and hide PMS hot spots, but don't use it as spackle that will rub off when you hug hubby. Yellow or beige undertones are best, but skip it altogether if you won't have time to blend, blend, blend. Steer clear of pink or orange based foundations; they out you as being made-up and belong in the kids' play makeup case. Two shades past your natural complexion is past the legal limit. Smooth on one with an SPF of 15 or more—a deep tan may look good now, but won't bode well for your empty-nester years—besides tans you can get

Poshmom.com Pick

Hands down (and never orange), Jergens Natural Glow is the best bang for your buck tan-without-the-sun on the market, especially for the multi-tasking mom. It's a double agent moisturizer and self tanner that will never leave you hiding streaks because you had an emergency, aka a juice spill.

from a bottle cause no damage. Plus you can't justify to your kids their daily slather of sunscreen if you walk around UVA/UVB vulnerable.

Test tons of colors before you buy. Forget your hands as guinea pigs. You need to go directly to the source, your face, and directly home afterwards. While you're dipping into the array of beige filled jars, never feel like you're being a nudge—it's necessary to scope out the gamut, and any salesperson who makes you feel otherwise should know that with your limited time they are lucky to have you at their counter at all.

Giving lip service

Line to give more pout—it comes naturally for your kids in bad moods, and on you it's sexy, not spoiled brat. Just above your natural line is the place to do it. Stray any farther and it will be clown-like, not cute. Bring on the color and get points for staying in the lines. Use a lip brush to fill in. Top with a glimmer that's not too sticky so you can still plant one on cute cheeks before you or they are out the door.

Bright eyes

The eyes of the Posh Mom are like a fair-weathered friend: they spill all her secrets, whether last night was late night (with your mate or a cranky kid), your next B-day is fast approaching, or you missed your last eyebrow wax. A PM knows just what tools to reach for to conceal (literally) her inner details, and when to enlist the help of professionals. If you're a waxing virgin, it's time to get busy. Brows frame your face and need to be shaped, at least initially, by an aesthetician. The results will keep you coming back for more; although with regular at-home tweezing, you can keep furry brows in check. Invest in professional-grade tweezers and reserve them for brows only—keep a second pair for household jobs like prying splinters from your little one's hands and feet.

Cheeky, very cheeky

Born to be bronze, Posh lives for sun-kissed cheeks. For her, blush is a has-been, even the word gives her the willies. She favors the bronze powders and gels year-round: in summer to rev up a natural bronze (from biking, beaching, and being with the kids, what shimmies its way through her SPF of course); and for a warm glow even in the dead of winter. We're not talking the Bain de Soleil model here, just a healthy radiance. So ignore all make-up artists, TV reporters, and magazine articles when the bronze is no longer beauty fads come around and they're spewing that pale is the new perfect. Untruths like that can cause a mother to foolishly trash her tanning tools such as self-tanners, bronzing powders, and tinted moisturizers, leaving her in a ghostly and a ghastly state.

Products formerly for your mother only

If you haven't smiled lately, you should. And you should do it in front of the mirror. Creases have stamped an indelible print on your life (and your forehead, and eyelids, and lips). You're probably blissfully unaware since you don't pause enough to admire your reflection that is a reflection of your job as mom. Being mommy to your minis affords lots of line-inducing "I can't believe she said that" smiles and plenty of "I can't believe she said that" furrowed and skin-unsettled brows, so you need to shove over the lightweight wrinkle-preventing miracle creams in the medicine chest to make room for a little tub whose purpose is actually to tackle those already existent—tiny as they may be—lines. Try something like Darphin Stimulskin Plus Eye Contour Cream for eyes that have expressed a bit too much.

Hey, Beautiful

So you're not nineteen anymore. Don't you wish that when you were, you had listened to what everybody said and that you were happy and thankful for the way you looked. Sure, you may have regrets, but so what? Fast forward to today—you are nowhere near U-G-L-Y and nowhere near in need of an alibi. All you need is to master your newfound hair, accept and launch an assault on creases and lines, learn how to do a Houdini makeup application act, and vow never to step foot in the SUV with a less than an apropos outfit. You're a little bit older, a lot more time deprived, but just as fabulous as you ever were (especially now with your majestic title of mom).

Chapter Five

Posh Home

I t's quiet. Almost too quiet. Taylor opens her eyes, scanning for the normal mayhem that is her mornings. Not one of the cute but typically guilty culprits is in sight. She wraps herself in her softer-than-soft sheets, fluffs her pillows, and basks in the glory that is Saturday morning. She's earned it after this crazy week.

Then her Zen moment is snapped by piercing screeches from not far enough away. She throws her duvet back, glancing back at her cozy lair and bidding it adieu until tonight when she'll be too pooped to fully appreciate its offerings.

Treading swiftly down the stairs (thankful that she put a snazzy runner down—the initial impetus for that dollar dish-out was so the kids wouldn't slip on the wood stairs), she still can't make out the epicenter of the noise, or its nature.

That is, until she spots the toys spilling out of the pastel-colored baskets on the shelves and onto the floor *of the family room. The path of Barbies, Tonkas, and stuffed animals of every species leads straight to her over-stuffed but sink-into-it comfy couch and the gymnastics show taking place on it: summersaults, cartwheels, head-stands—did she just see a back handspring go by?*

As she moves the theatrics to lower ground—a soft, won't-hurt-if-you-"tumble"-off-it spot—she is happy for one thing other than that her fancy sofa in the living room was spared: the fact that the noise that crashed her dreams was squeals of delight and not pain. Something definitely worth getting out of bed for.

For a Posh Mom, her home is her haven—it's where her family starts and ends their day, and where they check in during the moments in between. No matter the address, nor whether a cottage or a castle, she makes a place for her family that is well-organized (at least sometimes), beautifully decorated, warm, and just plain inviting, because for her, warmth is not a learned attribute, it's an inherent forte.

The organization part is what can get terribly tricky, especially when you throw more than one kid's schedule into the mix. It's easy to place blame on the kids, but the little guys can't be faulted, even if it was the two-year-old who took the invitation off the corkboard and turned it into drawing paper. A Posh Mom has to be vigilant in order to avoid such pandemonium, and she can start with organizing herself.

Mom Agenda

Pre-kids, the posh girl was blessed with the power to remember to-dos even if they never made it to her hand-written or electronic list. Now, fugheddaboutit. As Posh Mom, she has lost so many brain cells to carrying children (the brain strain worsens with every pregnancy) that she must pencil in a to-do if it's got to get done. She needs to learn to use that PDA she's been showing off (but has nothing in), or, if she doesn't want to trash paper for a Treo, then commit to that day planner and start to keep score of what's going on. After all, if you think spacing on lunch with your posh pals is just a whoops, it's way more. A PM always counts on her friends and expects them to count on her, too—even if it's just to split a salmon nicoise salad and the check. And there's no way she should over-lap Saturday night plans out when her house is the hot spot for her daughter's sleepover.

If that unthinkable happens, don't falter: cancel your plans in a jiffy, get in slumber party mode, and make a note—not the mental kind but the sticky kind—to head out and buy an agenda book or kitchen counter calendar first thing *mañana*. Grab one that's fashionable and fit for moms with space for yours and your kids' to-dos. Fill it with all activities and other certain-to-forget-if-not scrib-bled-down info like "who" sent a birthday invite, "what" to buy for the gift, "when" the drop-off and pick-up for the party is, etcetera. Then assign each offspring their choice of colored pencil so you can see who needs to be where in a quick scan.

Boy-oh Bags ● ● •

Walking out of the house (and the car, the office, and the preschool) with her bag slung over her shoulder is where the PM is the picture of posh. But she treads lightly lest she falter in her flats, her body stumbling one way, her bag flying the other, the jumble of stuff inside flying out. Remember when your biggest fear (concerning your purse, that is) was that a tampon would fall out in the middle of a rain storm and explode in plain view? It couldn't get worse than that, huh? Until you starting hoarding cheese sticks for after-ballet snacks and then forgetting about them, only to pull them out a week later to find they are not the tampon you were aiming for. Come on, now.

A Posh Mom has to overcome the ease at which she turns her purse into a traveling junk drawer. No judgment here—it's completely understandable. Always on the run and not wanting to litter or lose important items, she quickly but gently places (read: shoves) store receipts, multiple lists, tissues (used and new), loose sticks of gum, power bar wrappers, little toy trains, lip gloss, cell phone, and even a random telephone directory from one of the kid's schools. Keep what you think you may even possibly need (after all, it may take the course of a year, but you know you'll use most everything in there), but just like your head, compartmentalize your bag. Tuck stuff neatly away in smaller pouches. Try a cute bribery case filled with no-choke candies and gum, for starters. And make use of all the trendy zippers and pockets you've got going on. If you've feel like you've exhausted the options, try again. Maybe there's an extra zipper on the side you forgot existed that is the perfect place to store your kids' spy books and pens. Or maybe you completely ignored the fact that one compartment can house a water bottle you don't particularly want to carry into your very important meeting.

> ## Poshmom.com Pick
>
> If you've said "I do" to the to-do-list, vowing never to trash paper for electronics, then you need to do so in style, and not on yellow stickies. The momAgenda has space for your day and up to four kids' schedules. It'll keep your life in tip top organization and you'll never again have to hightail it to a baseball practice pick-up that you nearly forgot about. And for jotting things down on the go, Bon Bon notes by Bonnie's Style Press give your lists a chic platform with moms just like you (only skinnier because they are pencil drawn) at the top.

Still, stuff will compartment hop. Set aside time once a week to reorganize and plow through the stragglers that have stowed away in your bag. You don't need to carry their weight anymore. Relocate a school directory or other important numbers you need on hand, to the glove compartment in your car (but watch out—that's another susceptible junk basin), or to the electronic phone book in your PDA or your cell phone. Limit your kids' paraphernalia to one new toy per week (while last week's stays home). And, here's a doozy: throw out what you don't need and never will—like any receipt that's been holed up for more than a year—likely it and the store don't owe you a thing—and the postcard for a discount on carpet cleaning when you've got all wood floors.

The Black Hole in Your Bag ● ● •

"Can I get this?" "I want that!" "Please, please, please." No wonder your wallet is busting at the seams. Not with piles of cash (we'd be having tons more fun with this paragraph if that were the case), but with receipts for all the loot you got talked into purchasing, as well as discount cards, frequent shopper cards, store credit cards, store credit slips, and more. Then there are your own credit cards, your kids' library cards, and that list of must-see movies (six years old, not sure you should still trust it) for when you find yourself at the video store not looking just for Disney.

A PM long ago retired her one-sectioner wallet to the drawer in her bedside table. Don't give it to the kids for role play, as much as they may beg—use it to file store credits (we know we're harping on this one, but the store owners bank on ladies just like you whose credit slips disappear into the abyss of their bags) and store charge cards that get swiped at the store only twice per year. Here, they are out of the way of your everyday, but in safekeeping. When you need them, you won't be sent into a searching tizzy. For her everyday wallet, a Posh Mom does well with a multiple slotted style. Not only does it keep her beyond organized, it prevents dirty looks and choruses of groans behind her in the checkout lines because she's fumbling for the right denomination of bill.

The Hub of the House

Most moms, even if they walk right by their stove without ever feeling as if they should use it, make the kitchen the center of the household. It's where they hang their shopping lists and where they turn polished countertops into makeshift desks and art stations. Not to mention that it's communication central, complete with phone, cell phone, plug-ins, and recharging ports. Rising above the bumper crop of school notices, yellow stickies scribbled with random "can't forget" commitments, and snack bags that did not make it to the trash bin (which has not yet been acknowledged by her kids), the Posh Mom keeps this room orderly—or at the very least, she knows the order of the disorder.

Her first move is to create spaces for every item and function, because she's a firm believer that you shouldn't glitter glue where you eat. Drawers get put to good use—for crafts, junk, and storage containers, and she prays she doesn't have to yell "cease and desist" when a friend or mother-in-law attempts to open one. Cabinets should house not only plates but supplies—one should be designated for triage. Band-Aids, gauze, and Tylenol have no business hiding out in the bathroom when they will inevitably be called into use by bleeding and bruised children who find you chopping and dicing (or dialing) over the island counter. Save yourself the sprint across the house or up the stairs and tuck them out of sight in the kitchen.

And the refrigerator should be organized by age and height. Place water bottles, juice boxes, and foods allowed at all times at the petite posh eye level so they can serve themselves. This lets you avoid adding consta-waitress to your repertoire—just be sure to camouflage sweets behind a big tub of butter.

A Posh Mom's second move is to keep things in convenient locales. Her grocery list is in close proximity to the fridge, because when the O. J. carton runs dry, she's only got a two-second window to jot the two letters down before she's got to save the pancakes sizzling from beige to can't-be-scraped-off dark brown. And since there's always a fruit punch mustache, spaghetti sauce in the lap, or splashes from the "I can pour it myself" camp, she scoffs at the notion of a lone napkin holder device (stylish as it may be) set clear across the room from spill central. Instead she finds room for a pile of napkins as well as paper towels in a strategically located spot, like smack dab in the center of the kitchen table (she may go so far as to duct tape them to the underbelly if necessary).

Regarding the constantly ringing phones, our mothers had one up on us, since their corded (rotary!) phones had a home on the kitchen counter. Not only are we constantly paging our handsets to find out under which cushion they are wedged, many of us no longer reserve drawers directly under the nonexistent phone HQ for phone books. Take a page out of that old-time book, though. Because 411 (we're not talking about the scoop from friends here) can get pricey if you abuse it, reserve a cabinet for all-important numbers. Even if you haven't taken the time to consolidate, you can find the whole lot of them—in yellow pages, school directories, filofaxes—at the pull of a knob.

Finally, a Posh Mom insists on safety. She knows the importance of letting kids be adventurous, but she also knows that you need boundaries in a place that harbors many more dangers than just Cheetos increasing her thigh size.

> When kids come home they don't necessarily want to talk to you. They just want to know you're standing there ready to talk.
> —Meryl Streep

Knives can't be pulled out to be used as swords, spills aren't something to be scared of (a Posh Mom would never scream over spilled milk) but something to be reported so they won't leave a slick for little sister to slip on, and cabinet handles can't double as jungle-gym equipment to aid and abet in climbing and hanging.

The Bathroom Playground ● ● •

Even though their tub is filled with blue and yellow swirl shampoo and a zoo of rubber animals, your tub, as stark and un-fun as it may seem to you, looks like a blank canvas they can't wait to get their grimy paw prints on. So let them splash in your bath once in a while, but first play your very own game of hide and no seek for all items you hold dear to your heart, or your hair. A Posh Mom thinks nothing of sharing everything with her kids, but the exception may be her $12 and up bottles of shampoo. To avoid seeming selfish and the "please, please, pretty please" battles, make sure to keep such goodies out of reach and out of sight. And for safety's sake, hide that razor, too, which can be hazardous to their skin and the dog's wiry coat.

Makeup is a magnet to girls and boys alike. They're fascinated by these things that work just like crayons and paints but somehow are sanctioned to put on your face. Your glee at discovering the perfect shade of indelible lipstick will quickly turn sour when that same won't-come-off quality adheres to your vanity chair cushion during the five seconds you walk away to answer the phone. Ever on-guard for her fine fabrics and products, a PM is cunning enough to make a make-up box filled with lightly pigmented and no-stain cast-offs and stand-ins for her little "office" mates to dabble in while she takes care of business.

Messing Around ● ● •

If your kids are privileged enough to have a play space, don't make it a hovel. Still, this is the one room where kids should be afforded a bit of leeway in the "put your stuff away" campaign. Don't fret if the trucks go in with the dress up shoes or the trains get mixed up with the pink furry boas—at least the rug beneath is visible. While a PM doesn't want her kids to take any ownership in the dining room (too much china and crystal), she is all for their input in the playroom—literally putting the toys into the storage bins, that is. She ensures that the bins, crates, shelves, and closets are at pint-sized reach level (teaching them a posh lesson on independence) but she isn't lazy enough to make them head of maintenance for messy craft kits or other art supplies that could end up as a new mural on the wall.

Q&A: Amy's Crumbly Covers

The situation:
Snuggling with my peeps on a Saturday morning is like a slice of cheesecake heaven, even if the a.m. call time is just past dawn (really need to order those room-darkening shades). That my sweet husband is clear on the other side of the mattress and holding on for dear life to the teeny spot left for him is concerning, but, since sleeping in our bed is a no-no for our kids, deal-with-able for this speckola of time. I eat up these moments with them, and they love it—in fact, they can't get enough of cozying up under the blankets then jumping like circus performers on top when the "just resting" turns to "not tired anymore." This is even more evident when I walked by my room a few afternoons later to find my daughter and her friends kicking back on my king-size munching on chips and glued to the latest Disney Channel tween hit. Do I kick them out or let them stay put?

The solution:
Privacy, please—and a crumb free-zone—is how I feel, and I want to say "skedaddle" but I resist for the sake of my girl's rep. But as soon as her playdates are on the other side of the front door, I tell that girlie of mine

that as scrumptious as her squeezable cheeks are, inviting her friends into my room is so not kosher, let alone hanging with them on my just-fluffed comforter. (It's the one sacred for-family-only spot in the house!) In fact, I review the rules about which rooms are off limits for non-family members and in which ones she and her pre-pubescent posse can roam free.

A Place for Everything ● ● ●

The living room is the gathering spot for the family (when they're not eating, that is, unless you allow snacking on the sofa). Whether it's super formal or laid-back casual, it should never be comfy enough to allow brigades of trucks and parades of dolls to infiltrate—unless there's a prenup (clean up, that is) agreement and an assigned spot for the stuff.

And since they'll likely have more of where that came from, have plenty of storage in their rooms to stash it. Underbed drawers don't take up room space but they aren't best for a kid who wants playdates to sleep over and for who a trundle tucked under would work out better. In that case, place their stuff in bins lined up against a wall or stacked in a corner—colored or patterned cloth ones have a decorative touch so reserve the primary hued plastic ones for the play room closet. The best advice for the master bedroom is to make some room in there for your kids and all the paraphernalia that comes along with them. You may balk at this if you have staked your room for grownups only (they have the run of the rest of the house, don't they?). But how quickly you will rethink it during the first Saturday morning in ages in which plans for the day don't start until afternoon, when you'll want some of their toys in a chest close by so you can turn over, rummage for a favorite, toss it over to your little one, and quickly turn back over for a few more moments of sleep.

Poshmom.com Pick

In walks Waddajuice, and kids can roam freely no matter the delicateness of the furniture. The pre-mixed half-juice half-water combo is a health conscious and oh-so-neat answer for moms who have had it with sickeningly sweet sticky juices that can't seem to find their way into the mouths of babes. With a spillproof top that makes it a disposable "sippy cup," Waddajuice takes the fear out of combining kids and furniture fabric—and of pumping up kids with too much sugar. Get a case for the garage so you'll have quick car-stashing access when you're on the move, and grab another for your house for when your kids and messy little playmates are on the move.

Sure, it might cost more, but the higher price tag is well worth it when you think about all the rug-cleaning bills you won't be paying.

Traveling in Style

Home may be where the heart is, but it needs a way to get there. And that car must be worthy of a PM, mutually exclusive of any particular make and model. It has only to do with being able to offer a friend a ride and not being mortified by piles of wrappers, last week's juice boxes, and what feels like piles of laundry but which is actually a combo of dry-cleaning and yesterday's soccer uniform, not to mention crumbs galore. A PM fits regular car cleaning into her schedule and keeps her kids entertained in the process—either by driving through the car wash pretending it's a fun and dry (must never forget to lock all windows) water ride or by letting them take sponge to the metal in the driveway.

> A suburban mother's role is to deliver children obstetrically once, and by car forever.
> —*Peter DeVries*

Help! Domestically Speaking

Before the first load starts to whirl in the spin cycle, it's clear to a PM that laundering little clothes, straightening toys, making beds, and pureeing dinner are bigger chores than they look. Her own laundry pile is Mount Kilimanjaro in nature too, but it doesn't even matter—she's stuck at home all the time, tending to her household and her family's needs, so clean clothes are not a priority when she hasn't seen the outside world for a while and she's unsure when her next foray will be. Believing that everyone was overexaggerating about how thin a mom could get stretched, she didn't look for any help around the house even if her husband (and anyone else who has actually borne children) told her otherwise. But now she is good and ready to count on another body and especially on that other person's two extra hands. As the household director of human resources, the PM is the one in charge of procuring the best.

Live-in or Live-out ● ● ●

In the so-called stylish decades of the sixties and seventies, only those from the trust fund set had serious house help options The only person even the well-off mom would have live in her house was her mother-in-law, and even she wasn't guaranteed to kick in and help. Your mom was probably the envy of less fortunate friends even if all she had was a little paid assistance with the cleaning and a weekend night out. Today, though, you're not viewed as spoiled upper crust if someone other than you is holding your kid when the doorbell chimes. Lots of lucky (and smart!) moms get to decide whether to go full- or part-time, live-in or live-out.

Live-in helpers give you more convenience but also less privacy. Spur of the moment girls' night is not a problem, because your helper can bathe the kids and put them to sleep. The less glamorous crib-sheet change because of a middle-of-the-night vomit episode is less inconvenient when someone else is there to grapple between the bars with a clean sheet while you reach in to retrieve and comfort a needy little someone. But as helpful as that is, she's also hovering when you're having tender moments soothing your little barfer.

Live-out means a lack of help at that unexpected hour, but a welcome send-off at the end of the day, when the Posh Mom goes deep into family mode. Just remember that when you need her to stay past the normal appointed hour, you need to ring her up with enough advance warning before you enter the plan in your agenda. If not, be prepared for the inevitable: she says no can do. "Busy" answers can cause big-time friction—you're annoyed and she doesn't exactly have to be a mind reader to see (or hear) that. She needs a life, you know that, but regardless, you're in need, and since anybody who's a mom with help knows, this is not a normal employee/employer relationship. You need a favor and she's not making herself available. Warranted or not, you feel let down. Roll your eyes to the sky, then initiate Plan B—a second tier (but never second rate) sitter to escape harboring bad feelings toward number one and to avoid having kids tagging along at adult-only events.

Equal Opportunity ● ● ●
With an influx of immigrants to the United States coinciding with a generation of Posh Moms who proudly accept help in order to assert their rights to lives of their own, you may find yourself with a housekeeper from a region other than here. If their native language is not English, they will invariably come to the interview prepped with a sprinkling of pat answers learned from the unofficial English language class given to all recent arrivals by country mates who've lived here longer. For example, when you ask, "How well do you speak English?" their answer will most likely be "very well"—it's the first one on the chalkboard after "nice to meet you." Of course the Posh Mom is an equal opportunity employer, especially if the employee is willing to be spit up on regularly, but don't be blinded by her prowess. Test for her true language skills (imperative for the well-being of your children). With a happy tone and pleasant expression, inform her that you smell fire, and it's possible the house is burning down. If

the reaction is a nod of the head, a winning smile, and a "that's so nice," you know immediately that the only fire that should be happening is firing her, even if she does bake an amazing chocolate chip cookie.

Friend or "Faux" ● ● •

Always grateful for the help she receives, a savvy Posh Mom remembers that she's the boss in this relationship. A friendly tete-a-tete is certainly more pleasant, but she never lets it cross the line to true friendship. Still, it's hard to be the boss when the baby-sitter is caring for your most precious assets. What if a reprimand, however gently put, results in her mistreating those innocent kids? Could a dirty sink lead to shaken baby syndrome? Acting on paranoia, you treat her like family rather than the hired help. In turn, you convincingly allay your fears at night, believing she'll do the right things and always be good to your kids, thanks to royal treatment. And it's not just in your mind—not just once but many a time you can be heard telling her, "you are part of our family."

You see your well-planned protection mechanism as foolproof—until an afternoon when you make clear (in a family-like voice of course) that she needs to take your daughter outside in the yard for fresh air and fun. You return early and find the TV on, your daughter watching Dora, and your sitter chatting on the phone, pausing only long enough to say, "I decided we both needed some

downtime and it was too chilly out there for her anyway."
As you scrape your chin off the floor, you realize this family stuff has taken a wayward turn. Since your craziness is partially to blame for her comfort level, give her another chance. But first gently but firmly warn her that as much as you respect her, she needs to respect that you're the boss—of the kids as well as her. If, after this, you see so much as a tinge of an attitude that makes you wary, see her and her bags to the door and vow to do it differently with the next lady. There are plenty of sitters out there devoted to the kids, know it's their most important job, and show reverence to their employers: the parents.

Posh Picks: Tips on Finding a Baby-sitter

- PLAYGROUND STAKEOUT
  Plan a day at the sandbox for your little one with the intention of scoping out the area for any potential baby-sitters there. You're looking for the ones who have their eyes on their charges—and not their ears on their cell phones—and who are making sure the kids aren't going boom off the seesaw or mistaking the parking lot for an extension of the blacktop. Schmooze with one having top credentials (as you see it) and coo over her little one—then

wait a few beats and start the inquisition about her job satisfaction, her boss satisfaction, and if she's got any spare time for you or the need for more spare change. If the conversation doesn't seem like it's going toward her coming to work with you, as a last resort, ask if she has a sister with the same nurturing genes.

- BEFRIEND GYM CLASS INSTRUCTORS
  Often these high-energy, talented (able to jump, sing, and do a forward roll without so much as cracking a vertebrae), super sweet girls are college students (if you're really lucky, early education majors!) looking to earn some cash. Scoop 'em and book 'em to be regulars, whether Wednesday afternoons or Saturday nights, before some other fast-thinking (and desperate) mom does. Since their backgrounds have already been inspected by the class organizers, you can do the initial hire with some confidence—then ask for references, as you should *always* do your own snooping too.

- GET GOOD REFERENCES
  As a Posh Mom, you are selective about who you'll listen to. You're sure not to take recommendations from a friend or acquaintance who has employed

five sitters in the past two months, even if the sixth one is a gem. Some moms fancy themselves experts and dole out unsolicited nuggets, but little do these mothers know (and you do) that when she's at work, her nanny is slacking on her own job, finishing lunch in the car before she heads in to get the child from class, despite the fact she is twenty minutes late. Nix no-good sitter hunters off your reference list and stick to asking them for fashion and movie advice.

- RESEARCH ETIQUETTE
  Be delicate approaching those other PMs you hold in high esteem—they'd give you the Chaiken jacket off their back (on loan and in a desperate situation, of course) but could be very stingy about their sitter, given their need to clear out on a Saturday night, too. Let her know you have no intention of speaking to her sitter unless she's okayed the idea. And be clear you only want to know if her sitter has friends (even if she is so awesome you have visions of growing old with her) to recommend.

- JOB SHARE
  If you are only looking for someone to stay with your baby while you cart around your older kids to

guitar lessons and Brownies, maybe there's a mom nearby who's ready to say see ya to her sitter after the clock strikes noon. This could even be a double bonus—an especially exciting endeavor if your friend turns out to be one you've long admired for her amazing nanny.

Scrub, Scrub, Scrub ● ● ●

Help with the kids leaves a PM free for other pursuits, but top on the list is likely not cleaning. And why should it be? She is either holding down the job of head house honcho or another job outside her home, and hiring a cleaning lady or housekeeper to pitch in a few times a month is not indulgent, it's smart thinking. She could use just as much help scrubbing bathtubs as she could changing diapers, and she can rationalize that it's a safer bet to get the help, too. A quick once-over on the bathroom floor before heading out to a PTA meeting might not rid it of the mold and grime as well as a thorough scrubbing by someone who was there for the purpose. Plus, why should a rousing game of Candyland have to be postponed because dust bunnies are gathering?

Out and About ● ● •

When the landscaper comes a-knockin' and wants to trim a Posh Mom's bushes and hedges, don't let your Hollywood-tainted mind think it has to be a scary situation a la Desperate Housewives. And don't think that a posh husband needs to get involved because a PM will get taken advantage of—on pricing, that is. Any man who works with leaves, trees, and mud all day cannot possibly understand your dual sweet but savvy nature. Your smile and upbeat disposition is easily confused for someone who is easy to put one over on, and only your husband can attest to just how false a statement that is. So you prove them wrong. Do the deal-making about fall leaf clean-up or weekly mowing contracts—dare them to make their first ridiculously high offer, you've got no problem whittling down the dollar amount. In fact, you thrive on it—walking away with the satisfaction of saving some dough on the outside of your house means you've got more to spend decking out the inside.

Toilet Training ● ● •

Plumbers have given the Posh Mom a gift that has less to do with pipes and water and more to do with the knowledge, that no matter how low cut the jean, she'll never have to sport the dreaded plumber's crack. Yet plumbers, just like car repairmen, intimidate most of us with their mental storehouse of knowledge on a topic we admittedly and happily know zero about. A Posh Mom tries hard to limit her dealings with these people, not only so she's not so utterly vulnerable but also so she's not stuck at home during the way too long window they promise to hallow us with their presence. Since she cannot command a toilet to behave (toilet, kids—doesn't seem anyone's listening), she has at least empowered herself by learning to wield a plunger for when the kids wipe with half a roll of toilet tissue, and found a friend in Drano to unplug drains that have been victimized by tough doll hair. Armed with these skills, she's only forced to dial Dale the plumber once in a great while.

> ## Poshmom.com Pick
> Now that you've got yourself some help, give yourself a treat that will keep your skin looking good through your helper's days off—and prevent you from spending dollars (non-reimbursable by insurance) at the dermo (you'll need to save those to pay her salary). Dr Frederic Brandt created Microdermabrasion in a Jar just for us need-to-show-our-faces at the beach, park, or work moms. Get the same high-tech results as a doctor's office microdermabrasion procedure with this crystal-laden scrub that's a tried-and-true must. It won't break the bank—you glow girl!

Too Hot, Too Cold, Just Right ● ● •

Despite her self-sufficiency, a Posh Mom calls in immediate help when the thermostat reads the wrong temperature.

Too cold or too hot, it's all the same to her and means only one thing—more complaining than normal. Since her whining threshold can bear no more than she already handles on a daily basis, she seeks professional help pronto, even if it's going to set back her checkbook. "The air conditioning had a burnout" is the worst she can hear, as it may mean a long time waiting for parts. Rather than subjecting her family to the oven which is quickly becoming her home, she sends her troops packing for a stay with grandma or a nearby hotel until the air is flowing again. If the thermostat hasn't redlined and there is some breeze courtesy of Mother Nature, though, the PM considers cranking open the windows or setting up camp with tents in the backyard.

Outfitting the Posh House

Yes, it's easy to peruse the Pottery Barn Catalog or order online from this iconic, cool and retro decorating spot. But before you order one each of A, B, and C, go beyond the galvanized bucket (no matter how many colors it comes in). A PM is creative, inventive, and thrifty enough that she beholds the wonders of flea markets (only the ones with the best vendors) and weekend tag sales as forays into an entertaining day with the kids. Ever the PM, she doesn't rummage, but she spots finds and immediately recognizes their potential—that old towel bar hardware can, standing on its side, become a wall sconce for flowers. Old prints, set in decadent frames, can be relocated (or ditched) and a PM can replace them with her own family photos. She thinks on her feet (and with a kid on each hand) to create a house that's unique.

The Little Things ● ● ●

Because of a PM's attention to detail, decorating is a perpetual project in her home. By no means is she moving furniture monthly, but she is paying mind to the smallest components of her layout.

Fresh is best

She has a cabinet filled with vessels for fresh flowers, and she thinks out of the glass vase when it comes to containers. And *fresh* flowers are mandatory—fabric versions, even silk, are banned from her home for their tackiness and dust collecting properties, even if we're talking about a single stem. If it requires water to live, it's in. But a green thumb is a must if a PM brings plants into her home. No décor flourishes from the site of emaciated greenery that's made up of brown sticks where the leaves were supposed to be. A chic selection of potted herbs (perhaps snipped from a gardener PM's backyard) fits right into a kitchen window display and can actually be as useful as it is pretty. And if life gives you a bowl of lemons (or you buy them at the local farmer's market), display them as a festive, fragrant centerpiece.

But flowers wilt and schedules don't always allow for a stop-in for fresh ones—thank goodness a PM has a backup plan. Try a perpetual basket or container filled with seasonal findings that greets family and friends by the door: decorative grasses in summer, gourds for fall that go from Halloween well through Thanksgiving, winter berries branches, and spring pussy willows.

You're framed

Family photos in all sorts of frames are another technique a PM uses to make her house a home—and to draw the kids in and away from her more fragile objects on the shelves. Let's face it: children are mesmerized by their own images, big and small, old and young. A Poshie may use a variety of frames as eclectic as her kids' personalities to showcase a chronological grouping of their shots from baby to toddler and on (not satisfied with only documenting her kids' growth with the pencil-mark-at-the-top-of-the-head chart by the basement door every year). Then with just as much finesse, she groups a collection of photos from her family's beach vacay in same-same driftwood frames—she lives for harmony. But she would never bore herself or onlookers with full-color displays only. She harkens back to her gallery-going days when black and whites had an edge, told a story, and were dreamy, and she lets the dream live on on her walls.

Wall art

When there's a rainbow-colored scribble stuffed into a school bag or a taller-than-her-five-year-old tissue paper tree sharing the bus seat with her kid, the PM is considerate of her budding artists' efforts and is big on exhibiting them (although she's not above unobtrusively ditching the one-lined scribbles or thousandth self-portrait rendered during free time at school). The playroom or other arts-and-crafts spot doesn't need Van Gogh posters—it needs works of art from resident artists. But if the area doesn't call for collages and crayons, she doesn't force it, she just finds another wall that she knows the kids will see often—like in the garage, right where she pulls the car in. It's a spot they pass daily and she keeps a box of pushpins handy here so they can have a say in the exhibit's layout.

> Always be nice to your children because they are the ones who will choose your rest home.
> —*Phyllis Diller*

Pre-kids, the Posh Mom was flush with interests, and her decorating style in her childbirth afterlife can reflect that. A gal who was a borderline groupie for bands like

Fleetwood Mac, the Police, and/or the Stones doesn't have to fret that concerts now consist of Sesame Street Live and Disney Princesses on Ice. She can relive her past with a den or study dedicated to vintage posters, old concert T-shirts (framed or not), magazine covers, and of course, albums—you do remember those, right? In contrast, a beach going babe can make years' worth of shell and rock collections the only accents she needs in a seaside themed bathroom.

Kid-Friendly Furnishings ● ● ●

A PM's ideas are plentiful and constantly flourishing, but she knows she can't change her colors and fabrics as often as she changes her lip gloss—it's a much pricier proposition. That's why she's as sensible as she is stylish. Normally bucking anything vinyl, she sees the merit in a vinyl blend for the kitchen table chairs that, even though a little squeaky and sliding, protect her from walking on eggshells when she's serving runny sunny-side ups. The same holds true for her motherly sacrifice of favorite soft hues. As much as her eye is drawn to crisp white or buttery ecru for the family room just off the kitchen, the tint of chocolate brown looks like a better idea, given her daughter's penchant for Hershey bars and the wandering dark and creamy aftermath smeared on the walls.

Every posh woman can admit to choosing furniture for its fabulous form, with no heed to function. Who really cared in the days of NM if a coaster was a must because liquid could ruin the dining room table—it became second nature for you and your hubby to place one down. But now salespeople look at you funny when your first question about an exceptionally crafted etched-glass table is, "is it durable?" You're referring, of course, to its ability to take a hit from your son's toy plane crash landing after its flight across the family room. Rather than stopping the plane mid-flight, you're on a mission to make sure all new items delivered through the front door fit in with your motto of "kids will be kids." You can see by the bewildered look Mr. Salesman shot your way that he's all for roping off the room in order to preserve the furniture's integrity. No way, not for you anymore. You're a mom, not a museum curator.

Decorator Speak

Contrary to popular belief, a Posh Mom has no real need for a decorator, but she would adore one and it would expedite the delivery of her fabulous furniture and window treatments. Or perhaps a decorator is the speed aide she may need to narrow down choices: which tiles won't leave her bathroom floor slick and slippery after the shower (even though her kids would enjoy the Slip n' Slide feature every morning), which light fixture should go in her daughter's room now that the little one's reading and going cross-eyed from squinting in the light cast by her tiny gingham-clad lamp, and which wall units have features that will save her (and her kids) a trip to the ER because doors and drawers can't slam on tiny fingers because they're made with safety hinges.

She probably will have more success convincing her husband of the benefit of this extra expense by using a different form of reasoning, though, as he is willing to wait until she frees up space in her planner to do her own choosing, in order to protect his wallet. Try whipping out this winning formula to get him on board: "it will actually wind up costing less." An effective if somewhat devious way to play (are we learning the tricks of our four-year-olds?)—this is best achieved by pointing out costly no-time-to-think-through mistakes, like the farm table you bought to go with chairs at home, which now seats the stuffed puppies and kittens at a tea party in the basement because it would require not only the kids to sit on their knees to reach tabletop but both of you, too.

Never one not to be in the know, a Posh Mom has taken the time to educate herself on the subject. Many decorating terms come to us from France and other fancy-schmancy spots, so you don't want to seem *tres* American and massacre their pronunciations—or worse yet, assume something is a covering for your window only to find out upon delivery that it's a chair. The following helps you navigate in the world of decorating terms, fabrics, furniture, and window treatments, and will let you hobnob with the world of designers, fabric store owners, ladies you lunch with, and carpenters, even if you do have kids tugging at your pants during the meeting.

Backsplash (bak-splash)—The short wall behind a sink that's perpendicular to the counter.

Not a stroke the kids use in the lake at summer camp.

Baluster (BAL-is-ter)—The vertical support of a railing that's become a decorative detail all its own.

Not a pushy woman who uses chutzpah to get her way.

Banquette (bank-ET)—A long, typically fabric-covered sofa, most often found in the kitchen around the family table.

Not about all you can eat for $9.95.

Bergere (BURR-gzair)—A formal armchair with upholstered seat and sides.

Nothing to do with a burger bought in gay Paris.

Chinoiserie (sheen-waz-REE)—An artistic style using iconic Chinese motifs or icons.

Commonly mistaken for a country that is part of the China republic.

Coffered (COUF-ered)—An elegant architectural detail, typically in the ceiling of a well-bred living room.

Not at all deserving of its deadly connotation.

Decoupage (day-koo-PAZH)—From arts and crafts 101, this technique consists of paper cutouts and layers of glue, lacquer, or varnish to cover any surface, like a desk or galvanized bucket for a trash bin.

Not your dictatorship being overthrown by your kids.

Faux (foe)—A highbrow way to say "fake," as in fur or finish.

Not the foe it sounds out to be, but actually friendly to your wallet.

Feng shui (fung-shwee)—A Chinese decorating technique that's all about harmony and centering—even for stuff that's not in the middle of the room.

Not the appetizer that goes along with Chow Fun at Shanghai Gourmet.

Gilt (gilt)—Covering plain-Jane items, like a mirror frame, with gold to give it a little glam.
Unrelated to what your kids give you on the way out the door Saturday night.

Grasscloth (gras-cloth)—This delicate woven design is used as wall paper (not wise for walls that see a lot of toy car traffic).
Not cuttings from your lawn glue-gunned onto fabric.

Highboy (hi-boy)—Reminiscent of your posh grand-mother's house, a tall chest of drawers with old-fashioned legs at the base.
Not your son swinging from a dining room light fixture.

Jabou (jza-boe)—The vertical partner to a swag drape—the outer hem is straight, the inner is deli-cately tiered.
Commonly confused with a karate fighting move.

Marquetry (mar-kit-tree)—Inlaid designs made from wood, shell, or ivory.

Way too fine for your kids and their felt tips.

Ormolu (OR-ma-loo)—Gilded metals, such as brass or bronze, used on furniture.

Doesn't go hand in hand skipping with "your darling."

Ogee (OH-jee)—A decorative molding typically around doors or windows that is arched with s-shapes around the sides.

Isn't paired with a sigh when the kids are rankling your nerves.

Secretary (seck-ra-TEAR-ee)—An old-fashioned writing desk that has a top portion closed off for books or messy papers.

Not the person you're looking to employ to make sense of your overscheduled life.

Shantung (shan-TUNG)—Usually spun from silk (we love the luxe threads), this nubby weave is instantly recognizable so you can pick it out from the crowd at a fabric store or your best girlfriend's house.

Not when you send kids to their room for their sharp tongue.

600 count—The number of threads per inch in cotton fabrics—the more the merrier and the softer.
Not a car-ride keep busy for your kids in the backseat.

Swags (swagz)—Drapes that are hung so that the design curves between two spots.
Can also be your triumphant walk when you discipline and it works.

Toile de jouy (twal deh zhwee)—Pretty as a picture scenes on fabric, from 18th century France.
Not the term used for the hard work you do all day every day.

Trompe l'oeil (trump lay)—Decorating's version of realism—painted on walls, screens, or furniture.
Very different from orange gelee used to promote tanning at the beach.

Set up house and home—check. Lined up mommy's little helpers—check. Decorated house and home (or at least started to dream about it)—check. Threw some French lessons into your day—check. Now, kick back on a chaise with a crossword and pencil (okay, dream with us on this one, but at least the pencil should be easily located right where you left it in the desk drawer, you organized chiquita you) and admire your handiwork.

Chapter Six

Posh Entertaining

The Saturday night get-together at Taylor's neighbor's house was abominable. Her oldest teased their middle. Her middle forgot how to talk but remembered well how to whine. The baby that she bragged about being potty trained proved her wrong in the pool. At the end of the day, when she thought she was out of the bad-behavior woods, two out of three were locked in the bathroom—their own doing, not hers—and they were "never, ever coming out."

When a paper clip successfully broke the gruesome twosome free, Taylor was anything but happy to see their little faces. Fortunately, common sense cut off the screech that was about to fly out of her mouth. Her kids did not set out to destroy the day, and the only thing that got bruised was her ego, so what could yelling and screaming accomplish? Scaring them, embarrassing herself, and perhaps most importantly, an eminent need to Botox her forehead. So she opted for an unexpected *response. No loud yelling, just a simple explanation of the possible dangers kids can encounter alone with a toilet and a hot water faucet. She threw in a kiss for each of them, along with a whisper advising that they had run out of cards to play with this dealer.*

Her warnings in soft tones, loads of patience, and maybe a touch of bribery have her, the Posh Mom, revered by all onlookers. Handled the PM way, everyone is happier, including her hosts.

Blessed with natural social savvy, the PM is hostess extraordinaire. Don't confuse that with being the perfect hostess, though—just one who trusts her tastes, loves to plan, can make decisions on the fly when necessary, and doesn't think she has to make more of a fuss than she must. It doesn't matter if she is catering to her five-year-old's pint-sized birthday party, surprising her forty-year-old hubby with a sit-down dinner for their closest friends, throwing together a last-minute barbeque for her best friend down the block, or having her sister and family visit for a long weekend (only when invited, of course). The Posh Mom manages to choreograph all the mixing and mingling while managing her daily grind: she juggles all. And she does it all under pressure—there is little leniency or sympathy given to the Posh Mom if she screws up the food at any of her fetes, even though she had the added job of overseeing homework while the quiche was baking (and then burning) in the oven.

Let's Celebrate

For a Poshie who loves to party, there are many occasions that call for celebrations, and other times, some celebrations require no reason at all. For the former there are birthdays, holidays (religious and secular), graduations (from preschool to high school and beyond), christenings, baby namings, anniversaries, housewarmings, charity fund-raisers, and more. For the latter, there are early fall evenings where it would be a social sin not to plan a dinner al fresco, an "end of summer" beach party, or a "let's get the families together for hot chocolate and s'mores by the fireplace this cold winter afternoon" event.

For those impromptu delights, you can strut your creative streak. And since you aren't constricted by a pre-determined date, you don't even necessarily need to plan in advance. Sometimes the hoo-hahs that come together last minute are the most successful, since there's energy in the air and expectations are nowhere to be found—Poshie revels in her brilliancy to pull out the chocolate Kisses for s'mores when the Belgian chocolate bars are M.I.A. But a PM is also skilled in keeping schedules and organizing details, and she does just that when it comes to shindigs that need to be thought out. She plans ahead when possible, juggles her lists, and preps before party time—allowing her space to enjoy herself and her guests (hanging with them, not just tending to them) on celebration day.

Who's Coming ● ● ●

Any PM knows that a good party comes down to a good guest list. The right mix of people will promise continuous and juicy conversation and earn you a rep (or renew it) as a stellar hostess. There are times when a PM just wants to hang with her close posh posse, and then there are occasions when she wants to send out a social all-points bulletin venturing past her inner circle. Designing a guest list for this kind of all-out bash draws on the Posh Mom's innate skills: strategizing, intuition, social understanding, and confidence. Snuff the doubting fire and invite that new PM you just met at your son's preschool—chances are she'll be as thrilled to be included as you would if she'd asked you—or attempt to make good with the mom you bickered with over your kids' long-forgotten (by the kids, at least) mini-feud.

When compiling your list, don't forget about "owesies." They're for the nice people you have absolutely nothing in common with but for some reason invited you to their bash, and in a momentary act of kindness, you said yes. Sorry, but if word about your entertaining is going to get out, they need to make the list. The Posh Mom strives to reach an almost-perfect balance of guests though, and she would never let her list suffer by doling out too many reciprocal invites at once. On the other hand, take your pick. If it would work better for you to erase your obligations in one smooth move, combine all your forced-to invites and create a potential matchmaking session among your "owe-sies."

Because the Posh Mom is intensely loyal and polished politically, she would never risk hurting a good friend's feelings by nixing them off a guest list. She wouldn't even hear of it. But the friend of your friend who just likes the notches on her social belt doesn't need to be there, so don't get guilted into including her—especially if you're planning an intimate evening. Hopefully you're not still stuck in "posh wannabe" mode, where it's hard to fathom that less is more.

Worse than forgetting to invite your very sweet neighbor, though, is not knowing all your guests' names and how to pronounce them (especially when a slip of the tongue can translate into a downward spiral of your husband's bonus). What to do? Tap into a friend who has had other social dealings with those guests and ask her discreetly to spell the name phonetically. Call the Russian embassy if you're not sure "Gallina" is pronounced Galeena or Galina, or assign the guest a pet name, such as "my newest gal pal" if you think she'd take to it.

Getting the Word Out ● ● •

Once you've got the people, let them know. Emails and phone calls are okay as follow ups to solicit RSVPs (so not posh for an invitee not to respond in a timely manner), but the paper invite is the first "inkling in ink" that guests have of a party to come, and the PM wouldn't miss a chance to make her mark (or help her child do so).

Focus on family

For a kid's party, the PM steers way clear of the party space-provided invites or the store-bought fill-in-the-blank cards, even if they do have those fetching matching thank-yous that could make life so easy. Not to say you can only go the special order route. Go to a store where they can add all the pertinent info via computer, and seek out an apropos card, whether it's one with a karate kicker or dozens of divas. If you're tech savvy and ready to take on a project, run it through your own computer. It looks fresh out of the envelope and enjoys a better shelf life on kitchen bulletin boards around town than one that's been hand-scrawled.

Poshie also spins great tales with more personal treatment: have your child draw a picture (of the party, of himself, or anything, really) and if he can, write some party details that are pertinent to him (ice cream cake with crunchies will be served and presents permitted), and you can fill in the rest. Then color copy the page, fold it into an envelope, stamp it, and send it. Praise his creativity and penmanship, just do a quick sneak peek to make sure it's legible—fielding phone calls with where and when questions or having to follow up with your own calls dispensing the right 411 is simply bad form and not good use of your limited time.

For the grown-ups
Regarding your own friends, if it's just a few pals for dinner, then dialing is A-OK. (Electronic messaging is only tolerated for last-minute girls' nights, when you're meeting up for dinner or the latest Kate Hudson flick as soon as your hubbies get home and the child-duty baton has at long last been passed off.)

But if you're planning to whoop it up for more, treat guests to a more stylish approach in a formal invitation. A PM thinks herself

Poshmom.com Picks

Customized M&M's from mymms.com can be used as an ultra-creative invite or a cool post-party treat that tastes yummy and comes complete with your extra special signature. You choose the colors, a message (to go on one side, the famous "m" goes on the other), and they'll even pack them in cute containers. Mix different pinks and purples for your little girl's birthday favor and post phrases like "peace out" and "sweet on me." Make an orange and white mix to create a Halloween soiree invite that's way more fun than any store-bought one, or announce the new addition to your family in an extra tasty way with baby pink or light blue.

fancy but doesn't make believe she's royalty with gold-laden borders and too proper wording. She would institute her own creative vision, such as a poem that reads: "At 8 when the kids are off to bed, head over to the Smith's for a great bottle of red." Print that on a long skinny card rather than a staid square one, and she's good to mail.

Get back to me now, please!

Don't flip if people don't heed your request for an RSVP. But have no shame contacting those who inevitably don't let you know in time—blame it on the caterer who needs to know how many lamb chops to order or the party space who is counting heads for place settings. You can make phone calls a day or two after a missed date and politely ask for replies. And be prepared to magnanimously forgive moms who are living the same crazy reality as you!

Broadcast the Details ● ● •

Ever mindful of her guests, a PM gives plenty of notice when she sends invites, and she's crystal clear in her invites about the details: time, location, and attire. As hostess, she gives her guests the same heads-up on dress code that she'd appreciate. You would d-i-e if you strutted into you neighbor's BBQ clad in vintage shorts and a bright white wifebeater (we know, terrible name, but so cute with a tan and toned shoulders) when a once over the crowd reveals one Posh Mom more decked out than the other. First you're panicked, then you're pissed: for you, barbeque is synonymous with casual unless otherwise stated. No one mentioned the five-piece band or the team of chefs flown in from Texas wielding the tongs. And stress sneakers if that's the order of the day, cause well dressed doesn't mean overdappered, it means just right.

A Posh Mom is also not fond of reading between the lines (she does not go for passive aggressive behavior in friends, mates, teachers, and the like) and would never expect her invitees to do so. For your parties, you also need to be clear about the timing—when it's called for and when you expect people to leave. This is especially true for overzealous partygoers who wouldn't feel any discomfort in asking your kids to pass the cereal at the breakfast table the next morning: obviously, your husband's boss and his wife don't know the meaning of fashionably late when their 6:00 arrival for a 6:30 party finds you still in final stages of primping.

Keep in mind that guests have expectations in line with your time choice, so don't let them down. A cocktail party or a champagne brunch mean just that. Anything undefined for 7:00 p.m. or later means that guests will be awaiting dinner, so don't leave them bibbed up and rearing to go (much like a newborn who is one second past feeding time).

Plan it, Poshie ● ● ●

Still, you need to know that throwing a bash is not all fun and no work. It takes plenty of that, and time to boot. Since time is most likely something you probably don't have tons of, make sure you're committed, or the proof will be in the pudding—or cupcakes, or tiramisu, if you're an adventurous posh pastry chef. Your stress will come straight through your tightly pursed lips, and that's the worst thing you can do for creating lipstick bleed lines. Know what you want to handle with your own two hands and what you want to delegate, and enlist the help of others to create and execute a menu (a friend who has every recipe she's ever seen filed in her brain), photograph the day (husband or brother-in-law who would be just idly standing by otherwise), set up (hire a crew), clean up (delegate to grandpa to keep him on his toes instead of horizontal and napping on the sofa), and entertainment (unless you've got a friend who does something she earns cash for, bring in a real pro).

As hostess for a gathering of grown-ups, a Posh Mom is not afraid of rolling up her sleeves (pre-"final outfit change") and putting her hands to work (if they are freshly manicured, a pair of gloves should not be pooh-poohed). If it is an impromptu to-do, like a last-minute game night whipped up because she and her mate have already exhausted the pickings of good new releases, she just pulls from her stash of ideas, best order-in spots, and good friends, then relies on her innate party skills to get the job done. Depending on the caliber of guests, she institutes a beer or whiskey tasting. She pilfers from her kids' game closet to pull out Pictionary, Trivial Pursuit (you might need to invest in the eighties edition—the past years have been busy ones), or video games to host a PlayStation tournament. And there's never too many cooks in the kitchen when she gathers friends together to sip wine and sauté.

For a premeditated event, the planning involves lists, organization, and logistics. If you're having just a few couples over for cocktails, your home will do. If a larger crowd can't be accommodated or if you'd just rather not offer up your new living room rug as a sacrifice to the evils of red wine, start searching for locations that would be second best, like the restaurant where the proprietor knows you by name and could be coaxed, charmed, or cashed into foregoing his Saturday night crowd for his "best customer" and some of your friends. Maybe the occasion calls for a picnic at the beach or park (just check if you need a permit), where the landscape is free and the fauna is fantastic—just be sure to pack the little posh details: a quintessential red-and-white checkered blanket (not a holey, oversized beach towel), melamine plates so that greasy, floppy paper ones are nowhere to be found, and cups for pouring water, even if the bottles are Evian.

Pay attention to the details beforehand—planning ahead and being beyond prepared is key for this type of entertaining. That doesn't mean you've got to start cooking and freezing months before your intended company is ringing the bell. Instead, employ some simple but tasteful shortcuts that will make the details look like they took lots of thought, time, and energy, when it was really just the thought that counted.

Don't chop the onions, roast the garlic, peel the tomatoes, and cook the meat for meatballs marinara when you have gymnastics class for your daughter ending and your son's piano lesson beginning. Instead of creating both meatball and sauce from scratch, pick one thing that you can get a handle on to home cook. Leave the rest to that gourmet store in town that does everything so right. You could still become famous for your meatballs without any of your guests knowing the sauce is store-bought. Loved ones won't be disappointed; they'll be thrilled to have the extra time to spend with a relaxed and splatter-free you.

And if a certain well-established Poshie in town is always using calligraphy on her place cards, don't waste your time, or worse, be dubbed a copycat. Set your table with clever pre-printed cards that read "reveal something about yourself to the person on your left" or "do you know the middle name of your right-side companion?" Not only will you be oh-so-clever, you will have instituted a no-lull-in-the-conversation guarantee.

Happy Happy Birthday, Baby

A Posh Mom never expects her kid's birthday bash to be the soiree of the century. Entertaining with (and forking out the bucks for) simultaneous pony rides, magic shows, and a mini amusement park might be the dream for her petite posh, but she knows it would be overkill, tacky, and something she would never ever want to have to top the next year. She prefers sliding by with a bash that's easy on herself, tons of fun, and all about her little one. That's the best way to make all the decisions no-brainers and bank on the guest of honor having a blast (that is, until he frets that his friend got more turns on the zip line or she cries because she wanted the purple flower, not the pink, from the cake).

Hope to See You There ● ● •

When kids are little, a party for them is a wonderful excuse to see friends and enjoy watching each other's little rugrats running amok. This is especially true for friends who don't live within a stroller's walk. But as time moves on, so does the need for your kids to share their birthday with children they don't know and could care less about. Your kid has been plotting the logistics of this party since the moment his last one ended, so why should it be infiltrated by virtual strangers he sees only two times a year? The answer is, it shouldn't. Trust us. No one will be insulted. They'll probably be happy not to have to attend another weekend birthday bash—wouldn't you? You'd be better served by inviting those same friends to an adults only outing on a Saturday night when all the focus isn't on your princess Peyton who wants (and deserves) a film documentary made of every tumble, cartwheel, and balance beam move she makes.

Plus, that leaves more room for inviting kids who should be there. Believe it or not, the schools' powers-that-be may dictate your kid's invitees for the sole reason of social fairness. For a Posh Mom who is sensitive to others' feelings (and is instilling the same quality in her children), she sees no need to buck tradition in this instance, understands these policies, and abides by them. There is no reason to leave anyone out, even if your child has dubbed a little boy in his class as "the scratcher" on the playground. As any PM knows, first friends are fairweathered, and "the scratcher" may be next week's best friend when he stops dabbling in violence.

> I suppose I never realized it before. Babies aren't really born of their parents, they're born of every kind word, loving gesture, hope, and dream their parents ever had. Bliss.
> —Julia Roberts

As kids get older, the move to break away from long guests list is set in motion, and celebrations fueled by their selection of friends, interests, and personality are the rage (ooh, the budding of a posh persona). A Posh Mom is tickled to see the independence blossoming and will swallow her reservations and let Johnny Classmate attend the bash, even though she's well aware that he's the back of the bus sex educator who informed her little sweetie that a condom is a balloon for a special place.

Q & A: Amy's favor for a friend

The sitch:
Two secs before our family is out the door, scrambling for the SUV with birthday partying on their minds (my oldest daughter's fourth), the phone rings. On the other end is a M.I.A. RSVP, who says her daughter will be joining the troops. Fabulous—it's not really helpful that she so stupefyingly blew-off my yes/no date (that passed three weeks ago, if anyone's counting), which was directly correlating with the favor company's deadline for personalizing the jewelry boxes. I was stuck with nothing to hand off to this child. Do I let the kid suffer for her mother's extreme party indiscretion, or do I kick my ingenuity into high gear (after all, I'm not focusing on everything else like pizza delivery, balloons, or Cinderella's on-time arrival) and figure out a favor?

The solution:
That a child is being reared by a mother who waited this long to correct a faux pas (we all miss response

dates, but the day of? Come on, now), is punishment enough. I didn't fret that she wouldn't have a box with her call letters painted on, and instead I got her the next best thing (or the closest I could muster up). On the way to the party place, we stopped by the supermarket, and I put together a package of markers and coloring books (making myself a little more crazy, I had to find ones in line with the princess paper goods my little one picked out). Then I put on my sweetest smile to prepare for other mini ravers to ask where their art favor was.

Chuck E. Makes Great Cheese... ● ● •

...and puts it on pizza. To guarantee success, seek professional help whenever possible. (Sure, a little Xanax would work too, but that's not where we're going here, sorry.) Tried-and-true party spots around town are host to tons of tot celebrations per weekend and have the formula perfected. For one, Chuck is a mouse that throws a mean party that includes food, band entertainment (even if it is by automated life-sized stuffed animals) and arcade games for every age and interest. Parties at this venue are a lot more affordable than his original rodent counterpart that lives in the land (or world) of Disney.

American Girl fulfills every girl in America's dream of tea parties and life with a silver spoon. Just make sure she knows before she steps inside that teahouse that parties cost a small fortune and so do the dolls and accessories, so she's not getting both. This will prevent her begging to no avail for a baby and a miniature car seat on her special day.

Tumble gyms in town give permission for tots to run, pole vault, and flip to expend an hour's worth of that pent-up energy all kids harbor. An added bonus: they also have an insurance policy that your playroom may not.

Play it safe and put the predictable on hold (with your credit card). Then search out a never-been-booked spot like these:

- The boutique that shows up multiple times on your credit card statement—maybe they can stage your little girl's fashion show.
- Check if that indie music store would host a jam session for your son.
- Firemen with their trucks and policemen with their cars can bullhorn a party that's both intriguing and educational. They are pros at getting across in one sitting a message that we'd have to repeat ourselves silly trying to convey, such as "never talk to strangers."

If nothing hits you as a must-have, be thankful for forethought and head toward the tried-and-true you already booked—you know kids don't mind same ol', same ol'—in fact, they love it.

Now's the Time ● ● •

Booking your child's birthday celebration at a professional party place is good for freeing up your brain space, but you are at the mercy of their schedules. When you make the initial call, the time slots available depend on the ferocious pre-booking habits of overly eager parents. Don't let your kids down on this one; you've got to exert your pushy side even though you try to deny you have one. If you are lucky enough (and a bit overly eager and early yourself) to have your pick of party times, go for the one that works well for your child. If her finger is poking you every morning before the alarm goes off, book the first spot of the day. Or, if you know it will be a whirlwind to get out of the house early (kind of like every morning for school), save yourself the inevitable battle even if just for this one, momentous day, and reserve a later party time. But beforehand, make sure to do your due diligence with other calendars and events that may win out over your birthday bash, including the school-wide carnival or your husband's week-long business trip to Dallas.

House Party ● ● •

What if you couldn't even snag a time slot at Chuck E. Cheese? Don't fret, Poshie. Even the Posh Mom on a budget is skilled enough to turn humdrum into the party of the year. She's not above bribing high-school cheerleaders to hold a clinic, using long lists of potential baby-sitting jobs as bait, or taking a sudden interest in her manicurist's love life in the hopes she'll say yes to painting a party's worth of tiny toes the Saturday after next. And she's more than willing to sell her soul to fund-raising for new uniforms if the baseball coach agrees to hold batting practice for a group of seven-year-olds in her backyard.

If you do decide to open your home to your teeny-weeny guests (think about this one carefully, girlfriend, especially if the backyard won't be an option), you need to grin and bear it and be smart about it. Set up a party zone in one area of the house and bring it back to the state it was when you just moved in—empty. Be

Poshmom.com Pick

No matter where the bash is held (even if it was your last choice), you'll want the memories recorded. Take your tech-savvy skills one step further or start on your way to technophile with One True Media. This online video mixing spot lets you turn photos into pro-looking video montages. Bring your images to life, fade them in and out, and set them to music.

It's beyond user-friendly, and it takes less than ten minutes—about all the time you've got. So put another notch in your pretty Prada belt (you documentary filmmaker, you!), pop the popcorn, and gather the troops to watch your latest production, starring them.

prepared for mini disasters (also known as juice spills), be okay with limited-time chaos (just be sure to put an end time on the invite), and be realistic. No one expects tiny tea sandwiches with the crusts cut off (nor will most kids eat it). Go for the party favorite that's easy, comes hot, and is only a phone call away—pizza. Anyone who doesn't fancy it has to have an allergy to prove it.

Pulling It All Off ● ● ●

Speaking of allergies, the Posh Mom never wants to be ditzy about matters like this. So, since you'll be bouncing off walls slaving to your tiny guests, etch a deep mental note or put ink to paper about who is allergic to what— you don't want to deny Timmy ice cream cake then find Tommy covered with hives in the corner (a significant mistake a PM should never make).

Convince your baby-sitter (with some cold hard cash) to miss marching band practice Saturday morning to help set up balloons, tables, games, and more, then have her stick around to help clean up so you can save your hands for hugging, squeezing, and playing pin the designer label on the diva. If that strategy doesn't work, be sure your guy knows the game plan for when he's not playing photographer, or turn to the unbusy and willing hands of a friend who has stuck around for moral support (as posh pals normally do).

Tending to the tiny guests who aren't your descendants ranks high on the importance scale, too. Focus on your offspring certainly, but set your peripheral vision to zone in on those you invited, especially when their parents heeded your "drop-off" offer and ran. Shy ones might shed their frown when treated to a little hand holding, like the cousin who knows no one but the birthday boy or girl and wants to stay affixed to your side until he feels comfy. Even the most outgoing kids might surprise you and transform into introverts—can that really be your daughters' best bud clammed up on the sidelines, the one who never seems to zip it when buckled in the backseat of your car? Turns out she's shy when your kid isn't just focused on her. Here's a prime time to extol the virtues of stroking others' feelings to your kids (promise a few extra minutes of new-present play time before bed if he obliges)—it's never too early to cultivate and harvest posh behavior.

> All that I am or ever hope to be, I owe to my angel mother.
> —Abraham Lincoln

Make sure you inform party instructors or entertainers of any special circumstances, such as no balloon popping for the toddling group, who might be surprised by the noise and set into a frenzy of waterworks. Tell the musician that your son is itching for a solo or the gym instructor that your daughter is more likely to take part if she's encouraged by the female teacher rather than the male. And assign somebody to capture it all on film (moving and still) since there's no way you want to miss a moment and you surely won't catch it all in real time.

Playing with the Big Boys

From the second the grown-up party kicks into gear, a Posh Mom is in the throes of graciousness. She orchestrates it so everyone has a drink (filled to the brim, of course), is in the path of passed hors d'oeuvres, and knows or has been introduced to at least one other person. You should be circulating so that everyone gets a piece of you, if only for a sec, and your man should be making the rounds, too. Assign a big-mouthed pal (only in the best sense of the word) to make sure conversations are flying. But you and she should never be seen huddled in the corner together, even if it's just an innocent check in and regroup. Guests may assume they're the topic of your conversation, and paranoia, justified or not, can turn your upbeat party into a downer quicker than you can pop in a pig in a blanket (a comfort food turned swanky).

You Shouldn't Have ● ● •

Of course they should have. When the occasion calls for gift-bearing guests, try not to look them up and down if they appear to have arrived empty handed. Even a small but very tasteful (aka pricey) token is always appreciated.

And a thank-you is always in order. Not just as you delicately tug what you know to be a generous spa day certificate from your good friend's clutches, but in the days after when you sit down to write a note. Make it personal. Another Poshie out there put thought into her gift and will appreciate that you really liked it—and it also saves your butt from an accidental sighting of a carbon copy note you sent en masse. If you're an uber-philanthropic Poshie, ask on the invitations that in lieu of gifts people donate to your favorite cause (listed so no money goes to Save the Seals when you really want to Save the Children).

For Others

Volunteering in her community is most important to a Posh Mom, as is helping others. She is involved in at least one charity and likely more. Because a PM is a pro at ingratiating herself and finessing others to do some donating, she will undoubtedly find herself on the organizing committee of any fund-raising ball, golf tournament, art auction, or carnival that's in the works. She'll have fun, fun, fun if her budget's on par with a Hollywood production, but for the most part, they say it ain't so. It's here, then, that a PM needs to use her panache and shopping skills to create a fabulous event on a shoestring so as much money as possible goes to those who need it most.

Invitations need to go out well ahead of schedule so she nabs the people willing to give of their time and their wallets (they're probably already being stalked by other heads of fund-raising affairs). People don't expect to pay without play, though—otherwise they would have sent a donation through the mail and stayed home to put their kids to bed.

For starters, there is a menu to pick. A Posh Mom is not a cheapskate, but for the sake of charity, she may choose to cheap out. And she's not too shy to tell the caterer that she wants ingredients that reek gourmet but that don't run up too hefty a tab, like sun dried tomatoes or capers. She's got the entertainment to budget in, after all.

And if there's a promise to be entertained, you need to give them a show. You've got a rep to protect, so don't use the magic genie who twisted a fabulous doggie balloon for little Hayley's birthday and insists he can do grown-up friendly designs. Also, make a rule to ban friends from showcasing their "talents" even if they profess to be the most gifted people you know.

Instead, search out the magicians who never deal in the animal balloon trade. Some have really stepped up their acts and provide a great diversion to keep guests from tiring of the bite-sized crab cakes. How to tell the difference? In the interview the genie must vow to refrain from a rabbit pulled out of his hat. He'll be required to wow you with some mind-bending techniques (how do those interlocked rubber bands mysteriously come apart?), and only then can he perform at your function.

If magic's not your thing, try reliable tunes: singing and dancing are synonymous with gala, and many professionals will lower their sky high bar-mitzvah/birthday rate when they know that at least a charity will profit. Not into the noise? Tarot cards readers make for some spooky entertainment and can serve as persuasion of potential donors. The fortuneteller may subtly suggest that party attendees part with contents of their wallet as per their passed-on grandmother, who just came through.

Silent auctions—or loud and robust ones—can rack up tons of money for a cause. A PM snaps up this position—she loves any excuse to hit the stores in town, even if it's for donations and not for selfish pursuits. Just because a Posh Mom is not handing over *her* Amex this time, a flash of her sparklin' smile and all of her previous "frequent shopper miles" put her in good standing with store owners who are eager to offer up the goods.

If she's not a slave to shopping, she can still sweet talk a select one or two shops that have her or her husband's

Posh Picks: Charities for Children

There are a slew of them out there, here's just a skim off the top.

Make a Wish Foundation

CJ SIDS

Locks of Love

Children's Miracle Network

Operation Smile

number (credit card number that is), like the jewelry store where the love of her life got the push-gifts for her children, or the sports memorabilia store that is solely responsible for her son's very complete baseball card collection. Store owners can even set up shop at the auction—the charity and the store share the profits, and she's not stuck running all over town to pick up the supplies. It's a win-win situation.

Read All About It ● ● •

All Posh Moms have a former or current friend who did public relations in a former or current life. Any of them will tell her to alert the press for an event like this. The Posh Mom wants to keep her social gatherings private affairs, but she also wants to generate big-time gossip about her fund-raising forays. Tap into anyone you know in the industry, and then woo the press—newspapers, local mags, even local TV are the most likely venues to pick it up. Remember that it's part of their job to keep the public abreast of goings-on. A simple letter informing them of your good deed and intentions should make them take notice. Some editors and producers may need more convincing, and small gifts, such as a tin of chocolates with the event date and time printed on the label or a small dried flower with the invitation hanging from the ribbon tie will woo them for sure. You knew you'd be a star, baby.

Sweet Dreams

A PM loves to share her home with friends and extended family. Overnight visits are a wonderful idea in theory, but in reality, they throw off the well-balanced aura—not to mention order—of her home. Luckily nobody's asking to stay overnight if they don't have kids (they've heard all the horror stories). Don't be insulted, it has nothing to do with your hostessing skills. A hotel is clearly a smarter alternative to an unreasonably early revelry call, chicken nuggets for dinner, and live entertainment courtesy of a seven- and a three-year-old.

If guests have kids as part of their luggage (notice we did not call them baggage), of course they'll want to stay. A PM's house is like a whole new toy store for the kids and a stress-free zone for their parents, since they may offer to help clean up but really can't, since Poshie's the only one who knows which clothes box is Barbie's and which belongs to the Bratz. What to do?

- Pack all the good stuff—makeup, fancy clothes that might mistakenly be used for dress up, and anything glass that was a gift for her nuptials—securely away.
- Pack the fridge with plenty of white grape juice (safer for spills).
- Avert a future brawl or any P.D.A. (public display of attitude) by stashing little Brady's favorite tow

truck that he can't bear to share on a shelf so high that even she'll need a step ladder to retrieve it.

• Prep the kids that since her sister tsks-tsks at chewing gum for their cousins, the sticky stuff will be off limits for them, too, this weekend—to avoid any sticky conflicts.

Gracious Home ● ● •

The Posh Mom is ever hospitable and makes her guests feel truly at home. The more the merrier, right? Sure, until you morph into a short order cook fielding more requests than ever, thanks to the insatiable appetites of growing kids that literally multiplied overnight with your overnighters. Don't get overheated—get sugary sweet with your friend or family member, explaining that not only is "*mi casa su casa*" but more importantly "*mi cocina su cocina.*" Then show her where you keep the PB and J, the O.J., and the M&Ms.

Duty calls in the guest space, too—it's the job of every Posh Mom to see that her visitors have what they need. Start with basics, like water by the bedside (a carafe and tumbler are way better than a kitchen cup when you can manage), an extra blanket or throw on the bed for fluctuating body temps fueled by going-crazy hormones, and the emergency stuff that will save your guest the embarrassment factor of having to ask face to face for something they'd rather not but unfortunately forgot. Don't forget to include a tweezer for splinters and for postpartum chin hairs that started to grow the second their car hit the interstate, a bottle of medicine labeled "drowsy formula" to get wired out-of-their-element kids to sleep in a strange bed (not at your comfort level, but you know others resort to it), and good reading material for once the deed is done. Try to read your guests and their tastes, even if that sends you off to Barnes & Noble under the cover of night and an oversized hood to buy a selection of Danielle Steele paperbacks that will lull them to sleep. In the powder room, place a pile of plush disposable hand towels in colors to coordinate with the room, so when guests wash up, they're not forced to use the same soggy towel as the person before.

Poshmom.com Pick

A grown-up hot chocolate made by famed pastry chef Jacques Torres—or Mr. Chocolate as he's known to his fans—is the poshest way to end an evening with guests. It's made from pure chocolate (no second-rate cocoa powder here) and you know it the second you pop the tin. For chocophiles, classic might be best, but if you're a mom who dares to be different Torres's chili-pepper infused Wicked Hot Chocolate is where it's at.

On the Road (or just down the street)

Even if you prefer hotels, inevitably some good friend will want you and your family as houseguests, and not wanting to repel her hospitality and suffering sticker shock at the price of connecting rooms so tiny your kids will be literally and physically bouncing off the walls, you accept. Oh boy. You can start giving the speeches about respect, politeness, and all that's posh-mannered now, but know that once you walk over the threshold, your offspring's behavior for the next forty-eight hours is up to nature, no matter how valiant an attempt you've made to nurture. Make the best of it with these posh tips:

- Come bearing gifts for your hostess and her kids. Make it something she'll appreciate—you know what it's like to be on the receiving end of something totally un-you. If she gardens, get her a galvanized spade and ultra-suede gardening gloves plus an herb kit for the kids and for kitchen growing projects (a step above an avocado seed and some soil). Or if they are film lovers, bring movies with a selection of ratings so after dinner you can split off: One rated G showing in the basement with popcorn, and a PG or R viewing in the family room with tea.
- Make yourself at home—to a point. Perpetually clean up after yourself and your kids, especially in the bathroom. You wouldn't leave Shrek toothpaste loogies and eyebrow hair in your sink at home, so certainly don't do it in theirs. Obliterating your messy existence will maintain your rep as a good guest and will protect your family's honor.

- Keep yourself and your kids out of as much "stuff" as you can. This includes but is not limited to the master bedroom, disciplinary acts that ensue between occupants of that bedroom and their children, the medicine chest of any room that you're not sleeping in, and the dog's biscuits (he may lead you directly to the jar, but he may also be on a diet that he's not telling you about).

- Don't let your family's "special needs" become your host's "need for you to leave." If your three-year-old only eats hard-boiled eggs, do not ask that they boil up a pot and deal with the stench in the kitchen curtains for the rest of the day. Bring a container of your own and leave the sulfur smell back at your house.

Posh Cocktails and their Classless Cousins

When out and about, the Posh Mom knows how to stop one from becoming "Miss One Too Many." She also is conscious that there are some drinks befitting of her status as cool and happening mom and other cocktails that no bartender nor living-room dweller should hear her request across a crowded bar.

Posh Cocktails
These classic and innovative drinks go down smooth and fit right in with a lady and her lifestyle:

Bellini—Champagne and pureed peach

Godiva Chocolate Martini—Godiva chocolate liqueur, crème de cacao, vodka, and half-and-half

Mojito—Light rum, lime juice, sugar, club soda, and mint sprigs

Gin and Tonic—Super premium gin, tonic, and a lemon wedge

Campari Smash—Campari, limoncello, and a lemon wedge

The Classless Cousins
We all have relatives whose blood-related status makes us cringe. And just like them, these cocktails have no place in the repertoire of a PM, no matter how good the mix may sound:

Dirty Mother—Brandy and Kahlua coffee liqueur

Redneck Margarita—Jack Daniels whiskey, triple sec, and margarita mix

Fruity Slut—Jagermeister and peach schnapps

Crack House on the Rocks—Black Haus and cranberry juice

Booty Call—Amaretto, Southern Comfort, vodka, and pineapple juice

Movies, cocktails, ice cream cake, extra comforters—it's no matter. When you are head-honcho hostess for any jamboree, you've got the plans down to the last detail. You wouldn't have it any other way. After all, why should you work your well-toned butt off to pull off the soiree of the year, then miss out on all the fun yourself? You wouldn't, of course. You've got as much as possible under control way ahead of time so you can kick back (though not recline all the way—you've still got pizza or passed hors d'oeuvres to oversee) and enjoy the par-tay with the rest of the guests you invited to hang out with in the first place.

Chapter Seven

Work It

At the beginning of motherhood, Taylor double agented as Posh Mom and overachieving career woman. By the end of the day she was wiped out, but she was happy to be wiping little tushies (and pleased she wasn't doing it the whole first half of the day). She maintained a powerful position at her firm, despite the whispers from everyone (except her ultra-supportive husband) and that the expectations would be too high to fifty-fifty it with mothering.

Just when her sweet pea turned three, a delayed "terrible twos" set in and the challenge began. Her daughter's normally outrageous and outgoing personality started to wane, and Taylor was guilt-ridden that this newfound "I want you to ask her for me mommy" attitude was somehow related to her absence at the bus stop, gymnastics class, and book fair.

Then one Thursday, when sipping a tea at her desk, she looked up from her papers and glanced at her

> All mothers
> are working mothers.
> —Anonymous

pictures. One was a silver-framed embrace with her and her little girl. She popped up and scooted off in a huff, hoping the rush would preempt her boss from asking for specifics. Even if he could catch her, today she was a woman with a mission, and she would not be cubicle-bound.

With no traffic, she made it just in time to pick up her baby doll from school, change her into a sparkly leotard, and stay around to peek in on the class from behind the curtain. Her daughter couldn't have beamed more. She was wildly showing off her "beautiful mama" to all of her little friends, and her smile made any repercussions at work worthwhile.

It was only the SAHMs who seemed almost disappointed that Taylor had shown up. Taylor was received at the gymnasium by a high-pitched chorus of "We haven't seen you here in so long" in a medley of disapproving tones. One mom even "complimented" Taylor for receiving a promotion as she simultaneously questioned, with eyebrows raised, "can you handle all you have on your plate?" Ambushed, Taylor found herself wishing she was in the safety of her office. But she decided to stop the chatting that was turning childish, and instead she *concentrated on the balancing and toe points that her angel was performing on the beam. The reason she was there was for her little munchkin, after all, not for the mean mommies and their snide remarks.*

But Taylor never forgot that escapade, and when, years later, she put her career down for a nap (never say never), she made it a point to make all moms she encountered feel accepted. Because office nameplate or not, moms are in a class of their own, and they all deserve class treatment.

Hi-Ho, Hi-Ho, It's Off to Work Poshie Goes

It's clear this generation has spawned some pretty wicked-minded businesswomen. Some have made the decision not to shelve their careers for carpool and bring home the bacon solo, while others share the depositing-into-the-bank-account load with their husbands (some even surpassing their sweetie's contributions). Many PMs stay their corporate career course determined that the sweat droplets on their fitted blazers will not be for naught. They won't allow men or hussies without kids to step on their slingbacks as they plow skyward in their career paths. Then there are those who can't be told what to do—by their husbands, kids, and certainly not a boss—and who bust out with a business of their own.

Poshmom.com Pick

The mom who works needs to do everything short of live her life in a bubble in order to stay well. Yet as a mom and career woman she's signed-up for the mother lode of stress. Vitamin C has been credited for reducing the effects of stress and for curing the common cold (which stress may have triggered). Emergen-C's Immune Defense formula contains the usual suspect of vitamin C as well as A, B, and D, plus germ killers like zinc and elderberry. The hefty dose of virus warriors is combined with a lemon honey flavor for a sweet taste that fizzes up in water and tastes almost as good as Diet Coke—but does a lot more for winning your fight against germs.

The Posh Career Mom has a uniquely harried schedule to keep. After the school bus send-off, she's not running to exercise but running to work and the pile of projects on her desk. Pros: she gets to fulfill her inner child fantasy of being a bigwig in a skyscraper or "playing" behind the counter of a store—and when she gets home, she hears the sweet "mommy's back!" Cons: she won't make every recital or carpool for every after school activity, which definitely sends pangs of guilt and sadness up her spine. But the Posh Mom knows herself like the back of her own manicured hand. She needs to do this, whether for herself, her family's bank account, or her children, who benefit from a more fulfilled mom. She exonerates herself from phrases like, "why am I the only kid whose mommy doesn't drive me to school every morning?" by showing up as a mystery reader in the classroom, with chocolate chip cookies to go with the book, "When You Give a Mouse a Cookie," and as a helper for getting in and out of costumes for the holiday assembly.

Whether working is by choice or out of necessity, the PM is a multitasker to the nth degree. Spurts of free moments don't come around too often, so she's got to dole out the minutes like her kids do sweet tarts (two for me, one for you). Weekdays she might be spotted tweezing eyebrows at a stoplight. In the comfort of her home after hours, she may, more often than before she combined kids and career, agree to a quickie with her hunk-a hunk-a burnin' love during a commercial break. Weekends are her saviors when she hopefully (at least regularly) puts work aside and dives into mommyhood.

Do You Do Day Care? ● ● •

Used to be, pre-kids, you'd have to quickly walk the dog or feed the cat before you headed out for work. Leave them home all day and they could fend for themselves, and there's nothing that you could be reported to child services for. Now you need someone or someplace ultra reliable to care for your little sweetheart(s) while you're busy doing business. Where to go? Your decision will come down to money and your view on childcare. Do you want individual doting and are willing to pay a premium for it? Then a nanny/baby-sitter in your home should be what to look for (see Chapter Five for tips). Or are you convinced that socialization from the get-go is best for your little bugger? Choose instead to look into a day care center. The options are endless and can be overwhelming, but just dive in and get going like the posh provider you are.

Posh Work @ Home

If Posh is one who works from home, then she has to really padlock the office door after hours so there is no risk of a body-snatching attempt by the computer. Office-going moms might think those with a home office have it made in the shade of their backyard oak tree—but what might really play out is a potential mistake if the two worlds are in too close proximity and in danger of colliding.

Think about it: if you're spied through closed French doors, deep in thought about your next email, your little rascals might interpret your temple rubbing as time to play fortune teller and stampede in with palms open. The wisest Posh Moms get smart and carve out a

> God could not be everywhere and therefore he made mothers.
> —*Jewish Proverb*

windowless cell in the basement (if there's room). Sure, natural light may be nil in that spot, but at least she won't have to lease an outside office space to get any work done.

Those smarty-pants mommies also know that if they are going to get any bit of work done at home, they need to employ a baby-sitter or nanny. That is because in order to concentrate or have any time to get anything done, the kids have to know mommy is at work and that there is another grownup on the job to read to them, play with them, fill requests for juice and snacks, and even draw baths when necessary. Any mom who thinks she can wing it on her own will soon be flying the coop when she realizes that "mommy's at work" simply means "our playroom has relocated to that room with the computer—pack all the stuffed animals/cars/dolls/puzzles you can fit into the wagon and let's roll!"

Poshmom.com Pick

The Butler Bag is stylish, soft, and looks like an everyday purse on the outside. Nosy next-door commuters would be shocked that you don't have your typical tornado of junk inside—that's because it's impossible. Strategically designed compartments make organizing a breeze (not 80 mile-an-hour winds), so you have specific spots to stash your lip gloss, cell phone, sunglasses, iPod, crayons, tissues, and snacks. When work is over and you transition into mommy of the year, you'll have everything right where you need it—and you'll know your bag looks as good on the inside as it does out.

Choosing Carpool over Commute

As a full-time mom, you need to consider what you're signing up for—guiltless pleasure in never missing a first word, step, or school play and raising them hands-on—and what you're giving up—a paycheck (down to one income), built-in adult banter, and time for your own pursuits. If, after a few deep-breathing yoga sessions (and countless convos with hubby and with friends who have been there done that), you decide to trade in your commute for carpools completely, then you've got your work (as rewarding as it may be) cut out for you. Talk about time management, schedule conflicts, conference calls (playdate details), people politics, and answering to your bosses, as tiny as they are. Took the easy road, huh? As if. Crack open your agenda when people try this with you—'nuff said.

> By and large, mothers and housewives are the only workers who do not have regular time off. They are the great vacation-less class.
> —Anne Morrow Lindbergh (author)

Still, staying home doesn't mean crawling under the rock of motherhood and cutting off all communications with your former high or low-powered colleagues. As a posh person, it's requisite that you not ditch people who were important in your pre-kid life. Make time to check in with your old boss, not only to tell him how your coochie-coo is faring, but also to let him know how you're holding up. Plan a lunch with the once underling who is now sitting in your office so you can stay tuned in, and make it a picnic—one you've packed—to get her out of the office and into the light of day.

After all, in just a few years, little miracles will happen called elementary school and school buses, which are like big yellow signals to jump back in if you choose to. When you make a point to stay connected, they'll actually recognize the number on the caller-ID screen and take your call when that day arrives.

Easing Back In: Part-Time Posh ● ● •

If you're that posh stay-at-home mom who gets a stab of reluctant envy hearing or reading about career PMs, then maybe you need to balance your diaper bag with a briefcase, even if it's just part-time. In the throes of rearing children you might think "where would I find the time?" but in a flash of a toilet flush, you're done with diapers, your kids walk out of the house with hair combed all by themselves, and they've tossed the brown bags for the hot lunch line. *Finis.* Lots of hours freed up there.

So start thinking about how to give your life that other dimension you've been craving. If you were the master chairperson for countless school fund-raisers, then you're likely zealous about organization. Get paid for this penchant for Pendaflexes by managing an office or starting your own party-planning biz. If you're done with kids and missing the toddler stage (but still want to be home to collect your big kids off the bus), good hours are the numero uno prerequisite for any job you take on. Try talking to local preschools or children's bookstores.

Show Me the Money

As we have hammered home since page one of this book, posh doesn't have to be perfect or pricey. Au contraire, *moi cherie*. An overflowing bank account isn't a must. One of the Posh Mom's most remarkable traits is how she can make so many pieces of her life fabulous using her ingenuity and a few bucks—not a few grand. By now you know what we mean: she can fly through the racks at Target picking out the basics, and use one good splurge to make the whole ensemble look like the shops on Fifth Avenue.

> A mother, who is really a mother, is never free.
> —Honore Balzac
> (French novelist)

Pre-Posh momhood, your home, entertainment, travel, and wardrobe could take precedence once the rent was paid. Now you and hubby are in the caboose of the money train, seeing it all sucked out the window and into cash registers at toy stores, drug stores (diapers, formula, wipes, etc.), supermarkets, and children's clothes stores. Not to mention the cash that you pay lactation consultants, the pediatrician (especially during winter months), sleep experts, and piano teachers. At times it may seem as though you need a lot of spandex in that dollar to make it stretch over every place you need it—and it can stretch the foundation of even the most secure couples.

In order to not rack up another cost (marriage therapist), study and put to use this piece of posh power: the power to say no. Not to the necessities, of course, they need to eat. But they don't need every toy on the shelves at once—do attach presents to holidays or good deeds done, not to temper tantrums in the store. You also don't need to sign them up for every class they've made a casual reference to just because their friends are partaking. Shelling it all out will not only leave you battling to balance the checkbook, but it will also leave you with spoiled brats who you will be battling with for years to come.

Q&A: Jara's Party Pinching

The sitch:
For my BFF's thirty-fifth, I was dutifully employed as party planner, inviter, and treasurer. I booked the

spot (a private room sans long table so everyone could circulate and chat), ensured everyone got the news, and got the word out that if they wanted to be counted, the group gift cough-up was $25 each. At the time, I was happy to lay it out—the dent in my bank account was offset by the choruses of promises to get me the money back pronto. When all ten of our other groupies showed, signed the card, and offered a hearty "your welcome" to the birthday girl's gushing appreciation, I was floored. Were they kidding? Okay, two of the ladies had every right—they ponied up their cash. The others were racking up interest and left me wondering the most tactful way to tell them.

The solution:
Money between friends is not dessert, I decided, so I lost the sugar coat. And I ditched the embarrassment factor of having to confront pals for cash—after all, they were the ones who left me minus the money. I kept it as cool as the cash I was aiming to get back (calculate it: eight overloaded wallets [with my greenery] times $25 bucks makes for a natty pair of boots), simply stating: "Do you want to give me cash tonight for the gift or send me a check tomorrow?"

Dollar Envy ● ● •

As the Posh Mom, have it or not, you would never flaunt it. But there are moms in town who don't share your philosophy. They have an obsession with finding out others' purchasing power and making public their own. You know the type: constant "complaining" that can be heard clear across a restaurant about how much packing they need to do for their excursion abroad, knowing the make and model and price of the thirty-six-month lease for a list of moms around town, and squinting to make out the etched lettering on the hardware of your bag. It all makes your stomach retch akin to a pregnancy gag. A PM knows the Joneses, but she doesn't need to keep up with their bank account. She's keeping up just fine, thanks, with the lifestyle that works for her family.

Disposable Income

All Posh Moms may strut to the beat of the same Cold Play tune, but that doesn't mean they reach the same notes on every score, especially when it comes to handling their bank accounts.

What would you do:

with a surprise $100?

Saver: Make a beeline for the bank. Ben Franklin's not burning a hole in your cargos.

Spender: Treat for lunch, get a mani-pedi, and stake out a shoe sale.

---

with a toy store credit?

Saver: File it away until the next class birthday party invite comes through the backpack mail—then use it to spring for the gift.

Spender: Use it as the baseline for an afternoon with the kids—scouring Geoffrey the Giraffe's aisles.

---

to save on a tank of gas?

Saver: Drive across state lines if the neighbors charge less—you drive an SUV after all.

Spender: Pump it yourself, you suppose.

with the hardcover *Olivia* book your daughter got for a gift?

Saver: Exchange it for the paperback version and a few more stories. Waste not want not.

Spender: Fall in love with that impish pig and order the rest of the books in the series—they'll look smashing on her shelves.

---

when a postcard announcing a sale at your favorite store is delivered?

Saver: Post it on your kitchen bulletin board by the school menus so you're sure to be reminded daily not to miss it.

Spender: Breeze in well before d-day, so you're not left with the sale scrapolas.

---

with hand-me-downs from your sister's kids?

Saver: Call them ready-to-wear (always the high-fashion-minded Poshie).

Spender: Pick and choose the cutest from the pile then go buy new stuff to match.

_____

for Saturday night plans with another couple or two?

Saver: Make the menu for an intimate dinner party at home. You're not shelling out the cash for the bistro bill and a baby-sitter when you can do the cooking.

Spender: Reservations at the newest, hippest (and typically priciest) spot. This is your grownup play-date and you are so worth it.

Working out of the house or not, it's got to be what works best for you and your family. Revel in your choice: You don't need to be an exec to woo your crowd or be elbow-deep in diapers to be the best mom in the world. Forget the code of those who do it differently than you. Pinstripes on a suit or on your wallpaper, it's no matter. You're still a role model for your children and on a fast-track to Posh Momhood no matter where on the work-o-meter you fit in.

Putting It All to Bed

So now that posh and mom have been joined as one and a generation has been named, no one can stop the movement from growing and thriving into a phenomenon. No longer can finding pee-pee drenched diapers, being overworked by big bosses or small, facing a disrespectful baby-sitter, or having a seam ripped open by postpartum bulge get us down. It may taint us momentarily, but we sleep on it and awake the next day to emerge as the Posh Mom we knew we had in us.

The PM's deal has been divulged, revealed, shared, and prodded, and you have a window into her friendships, cupboards, bedrooms, closets, even her underwear

> Children are the anchors of a mother's life.
> —*Sophocles*

drawer, for God sakes. But most important of all, you are privy to the Posh Mom's mottos—prudent pieces of a whole pie of posh life that will help guide you through yours. A quick reminder to send you off:

1. Live for your kids

No, not live and breathe *solely* for them, as cute and yummy as they are. But appreciate their misused words, record the moments of sibling tenderness (they may not be there in five minutes), plant a kiss any time they'll allow, and preach your love as often as you insist on clean-up. Never, ever forget that lady we told you about at The Gap who said "it goes by in a flash," and savor the tickling, tantrums, and total chaos—all with equal reverence.

2. Put family first...

As a mom, you have to prep yourself for a lot of things: for those times when the school nurse calls and says your child is doubled-over with stomach pain, for the day your husband is less than happy with his work, and for the inevitable conversation that begins with "a boy at school wasn't nice to me." Your mushy mommy hearts need to stiffen up quick and get as hard as your engagement ring rock in order to advise, support, and be there without hysterics as best you can. If duty calls, and only a Posh Mom can provide the essential answers, she cancels that facial, even if she knows it'll be months before she'll be under Olga's steam machine again.

3. ...and yourself on your to-do list

Don't set yourself up for the letdown of thinking you'll be penciling yourself in on an everyday basis. That would only happen if you are willing to neglect those little posh possums, and a Posh Mom can barely utter that horrible word. But do maintain a coveted weekly spot for seeing your name in lights (or pencil)—and scope out other times you can cram yourself in.

4. Be hip, savvy, and sensational

A PM lives for today and lives it up like no mom of the past. She wants the best for herself and her family and at the very least is in the know about what the ultimate is, even if it's out of reach—for the moment. Who cares that she can't afford the trip to Monaco, she knows what's up with Prince Albert and his womanizing ways. And if her little one is wearing a coat that looks like her mom blew the mortgage on it, Poshie will blow you away with the minimal price she actually paid. Move over, plain Jane mom, and let Posh Mom show you her fabulous ways.

5. Balance confidence and humility

Bragging is a holdover from grade school that the Posh Mom only talks about when it comes up in conversation with her grade-schooler. She knows she's living the life with a fantastic family and friends, but she's not out on a bullhorn telling all of the town's inhabitants all of the details. Her grandmother may have left her a hefty inheritance, but no one would know she has a pricey new watch on her wrist unless they spot it. After heading the Ronald McDonald fund-raiser and being honored by the Charitable Women Society, her humble response to the reporter for the local paper's question as to how she does it all is not at all focused on her ego, it's simply, "thanks to all the many people who made this happen."

6. Revel in the everyday

A day in the life of a mom is a good one if it's uneventful. No one smashes their finger in a door, a run-in with a mom who previously felt snubbed by Poshie is perfectly genial, the evening meal includes vegetables that make "all gone," the bedtime routine is completed in just under an hour, and there's even a moment for review of the day with her man. It's the little successes in keeping the daily grind to minimal pandemonium that have her feeling just dandy—it doesn't get much better.

7. Treat yourself to the fine things in life

With your funds tied into all things Disney and Dungeons and Dragons, it's not easy to justify a splurge on yourself, and very easy to feel guilty participating in indulgence. But if anyone deserves a power-pick-me-up, it's you. A fragrance may take you to another world (way cheaper than a plane ticket and a spa stay), a designer bag or a damn good fake can bring on a daily smile, or a weekend with your best girl from high school sans kids should resuscitate your worn soul. The Posh Mom knows that any good she does unto herself will come back tenfold to her kids.

8. Aspire to be stylish

Style is a Posh Mom's hallmark, and the work it takes to engineer it is well worth her while. She reads magazines, keeps her eyes peeled, and checks in with celebs (aka logs on to people.com). She sports the clothes that are downright appropriate and the few times she's a little off, her head is held high enough to divert any attention away from her faux pas. For Poshie, accessories are not voluntary but mandated, and she's up on which ones will keep her look up-to-date—not take her down to the brink of teeny-bopper party girl.

9. Make home your haven

Home as home base is expected to be warm, decorated in this century, and able to be walked through without a toy-induced stumble and fall. But it should also be lived-in—it shouldn't resemble a museum, complete with plaques threatening fines one will receive if anything is touched. Invest in some help in maintaining the balance: when the day comes that children can open a laundry basket, rinse a dish, and rake the leaves, they should. This will serve to prevent them from someday recalling memories of when they got away with doing nothing.

10. Treasure your friends

Let those closest to you know that while you're devoted to family first, you rely on them as a major support network and are there for them 100 percent. You don't need a posh posse of random look-alikes, just stick to the quorum of good chums whom you couldn't imagine living without. You're all busy, but remind them every so often that they're your best gal pals. Take care, though, not to lay it on like Balmex on a tushy rash—there doesn't need to be a weekly memo on the subject.

11. Be a gracious hostess

When you're entertaining, whether serving alcohol-infused cocktails or the virgin variety (apple juice, hold the spike), you've got to be focused on the cater-to-your-guest menu, not just the ordered-in canapés. Finesse the guest list, set the mood, work the room—and get into the groove yourself. Even Emily Post would tell you that social gatherings, especially your own, are not a spectator sport.

12. Get cultured, not pompous

The arts are a beautiful thing—and not just the colors fancied by Chagall. Theater (the kind with popcorn and those with ushers), the ballet, opera, and high-school orchestra recitals are enriching and rewarding, even when they're not a tax deduction. Spend a few Sundays auditioning different sorts until you hone in on what will make you happy as a group. Do spring for a season's worth of tickets if you can, or even attend a few random shows—it's something to look forward to, and the money spent will keep you from skipping out. Don't start theorizing aloud about what you've seen for any nearby ears (in a snobbish accent you've reserved for just this kind of convo). A show-off is one of the art world's biggest turn-offs.

13. Know your etiquette

As a PM, you're going to wander your way into situations that call for Oxy-Clear thinking and Ginsu-sharp reactions (you'd better start changing the infomercial channel) if you're going to walk out upright and with your dignity intact. Flexing your manners beats out middle-finger flexing all of the time, even though that bird has wanted to make a break for the North Pole on more than one occasion. Enlighten yourself to some Delilah Do-right diplomacies so being poised in potentially treacherous spots comes naturally.

14. Speak your mind

Saying "yes" to appease anybody is not the posh way. Sure, you've got oodles of opinions and should share them. And by all means say what you're itching to. Just be sure to edit yourself first—clear that speech through the filter that is your conscience before it rolls so (hopefully) eloquently off your tongue. Statements are one thing, a soapbox just for spewing is quite another.

15. Be graceful under pressure

Keep your cool, baby. Spit happens: someone turns down the volume on your clock radio so your alarm goes off at a volume that only the neighbor's dog can hear and you unwittingly sleep in. You have to pull out of girls' night out when your daughter's bronchitis wins out over your need to have a cocktail with your crew. Deal with the fact they're all going to wrangle you: kids, hubby, nosy neighbors, even your BFFs. Don't fret, it's only going to ruin your nails (biting, picking the polish, smacking the wall in a fit of frustration), your skin (stress leads to blemishes), and your hair (pulling it out of your head does not do wonders for the follicles). Not to mention the havoc it will wreak on your self-composure and your relationships. Counting your way to calm is always a way better alternative to yelling—and something you won't regret in the morning.

Anyone who balked and thought finding her posh couldn't be done now secs there's a method to maintaining and achieving her most fabulous self. You have to spare a bit of what's you for the quest to get your grooviness back in check. Delve deep into the bottomless pit of your purse to find what makes you tick, and go with it. Believe you deserve this preferential treatment. The dish on these pages is meant to be your instigation and inspiration—every point may not trip your light fantastic, and that's okay. Take what works for you and turn it into something valid to your every day. Because every mom is entitled to delight in her poshness—after all, she's got it coming to her.

Acknowledgments

We want to thank the many people who helped make this book happen. To our editor, Shana Drehs; to our other editor Bethany Brown, who was sold on the idea from the get-go; our agents Jane Dystel and Stacey Glick, who took our proposal and the Posh Mom Movement on; and to the other folks behind the scenes at Sourcebooks, Tara VanTimmeren and Katie Olsen. To Joy Wildes for her guidance and advice, to Danielle Monsees whose design talent gave our mental vision of Poshie a form on paper, and then, there's Starbucks, our very first office.

We also want to thank our loving families for their patience for the day we declared "we're done."

Last, but certainly not least, we want to thank our friends for their unending support—being the P.C. Poshies we are, we don't want to name names, but there are a select few and you know who you are—who are still returning our phone calls even after we went MIA in book writing oblivion as we brought the Posh Mom to life.

Power to PMs.

Photo © Cari Miller

About the Authors

Amy Nebens (right) is a former editor for *Martha Stewart Living* and the author of several lifestyle books' on entertaining. She is so proud to be the co-creator of *The Posh Mom Life* and poshmom.com. She lives with her husband and their three children in Connecticut.

Jara Negrin began working early, appearing in television commercials at the age of three, going on to star in more than seventy-five national commercials. An entrepreneur to the core, she has had successful publishing and export businesses and now has an unending belief in the Posh Mom Life and the movement sweeping the country. She resides in Connecticut with her husband and their two children.